T0321342

Failing Our Future

Failing
Our
Future

How Grades Harm Students,
and What We Can Do about It

Joshua R. Eyler

JOHNS HOPKINS UNIVERSITY PRESS

Baltimore

Johns Hopkins University Press
2715 North Charles Street
Baltimore, Maryland 21218
www.press.jhu.edu

Library of Congress Cataloging-in-Publication Data

Names: Eyler, Joshua, author.
Title: Failing our future: how grades harm students, and what
    we can do about it / Joshua R. Eyler.
Description: Baltimore : Johns Hopkins University Press, 2024. |
    Includes bibliographical references and index.
Identifiers: LCCN 2023058794 | ISBN 9781421449937 (hardcover :
    acid-free paper) | ISBN 9781421449944 (ebook)
Subjects: LCSH: Grading and marking (Students)—United
    States—Evaluation. | Students—Rating of—United States—
    Evaluation.
Classification: LCC LB3060.37 .E95 2024 | DDC 371.27/20973—
    dc23/eng/20240226
LC record available at https://lccn.loc.gov/2023058794

A catalog record for this book is available from the British Library.

*Special discounts are available for bulk purchases of this book.
For more information, please contact Special Sales at
specialsales@jh.edu.*

For Kariann and Lucy, now and always

Contents

Contents

Preface: Scarlet Letters

> On the breast of her gown, in fine red cloth, surrounded
> with an elaborate embroidery and fantastic flourishes of
> gold thread, appeared the letter A.
> —Nathaniel Hawthorne, *The Scarlet Letter*, 39

When my daughter, Lucy, entered first grade a few years ago, I had somewhat foolishly convinced myself that I was prepared to help with any problem that might arise for her as she took another step on her educational journey. Playground politics? Check. Mystery meat at lunch? You bet. Unfortunately, my hubris caught up to me with unexpected speed. A couple of weeks after the term began, Lucy started bringing home her schoolwork. Instead of talking excitedly to me about the project or the topic of the work as she had done in kindergarten, Lucy began asking me questions like "What does an 'A' mean?" and "Why does it say 82?" and "How come my friend got a 100 and I didn't?" Not long after this, she began a running tally of how many perfect scores she received on the frequent quizzes she and her fellow 6-year-olds were asked to take.

At one point I remember sitting on our couch and staring up at the ceiling. How, I wondered, had all of this spiraled out of control so quickly? As someone who has worked in higher education as a faculty member and a leader of teaching initiatives for 17 years, I should have seen it coming. I have certainly observed the damage wrought by our grade-obsessed culture on countless college students and their ability to learn and to thrive. What's more, I had just finished writing a book about learning and, as a part of this process, had read studies demonstrating the negative effect of grades on our natural curiosity and our desire to take intellectual risks. But it wasn't until this moment, as a parent, that I realized how early this emphasis on grades begins and how innocuous it can at first seem.

It turns out that spending years moving through educational systems that prize grades above all else has a profound effect on a person's happiness, well-being, and motivation to learn. Pushing back against this system is difficult but necessary if we are going to improve the lives of our children and to help them pursue goals that will allow them to define success on their own terms.

There is no shortage of problems to tackle when it comes to American education, so why focus on the deeply entrenched methods of grading and evaluation? It is true that we could turn our attention to privatization, charter schools, legislative budget cuts, teacher shortages, and much more. These issues are certainly important, but they have emerged fairly recently and tend to be more localized, either at the district or state level, though some of them do rise to the level of national concerns. Grades, on the other hand, are everywhere, in all types of schools. They have been around in one form or another for hundreds of years, and they're firmly rooted in our schools and colleges. While grades may be unpopular among students and teachers alike, their overall merit (or lack thereof) has not sparked the same heated debate as have many of the trends listed above. The more we scrutinize grading systems, however, the clearer it becomes that grading is a pernicious practice, one that is harming rather than helping our kids, and it should arouse much greater alarm.

Getting a good grade is supposed to be a sign of excellence, but research shows that the messages sent by grades are often destructive rather than constructive. Grades interfere with our intrinsic motivation and perpetuate the idea that school is a place for competition rather than discovery. Grades focus students' attention on rewards and distract them from exploring ideas about which they are curious and from pursuing the answers to meaningful questions, because there is no incentive to do so. In fact, grades significantly impede the learning process. I spent the better part of the last decade researching and writing about the science of learning, and one idea that emerges time and time again from studies in this area is the importance of failure. In order to figure out a problem or truly understand a concept, we need to play with possibilities, make mistakes, receive productive feedback, and try again.[1] Grading systems demonize failure rather than uphold it as a critical aspect of building new knowledge.

Even worse, grades are affecting our children's physical, emotional, and psychological well-being. Specifically, the stress felt by children, teenagers, and college-age students about grades, along with the pressure they experience from parents and teachers to excel academically, are directly linked to the widely reported mental health crisis in these age groups. Rates of anxiety, depression, and even suicidal ideation have spiked dramatically, and academic stress tied to grades is a leading cause of this escalation. We now have evidence in major studies from the Pew Research Center and other organizations that these health issues have been getting worse over time. I will have much more to say about these studies in later chapters, but for now it is clear that the situation is not likely to get better without some sort of serious, sustained intervention. A portion of our efforts on this front must be devoted to examining the harm caused by grades. They are, quite simply and without exaggeration, hurting our children.

Indeed, both inside and outside of the classroom, grades bear a resemblance to that ubiquitous symbol in Nathaniel

Hawthorne's novel *The Scarlet Letter*. Many of you probably remember reading this book in high school or college. Whether those memories are fond ones or not is a different question altogether, but it cannot be denied that the novel is a touchstone for many literature classrooms across the country.

If it has been a while since you have read it, I offer just a brief recap of the plot here: In seventeenth-century New England, Hester Prynne is forced by the inhabitants of her town to wear a red "A" on her clothes as punishment for what they judge to be her adultery and for having a child, Pearl, as a result of the affair. Eventually we meet her husband, who was presumed to be lost at sea, as well as Arthur Dimmesdale, the local minister, who (spoiler alert!) turns out to be the father of Pearl. Dimmesdale is racked with guilt, which he—because he is a man—is allowed to suffer mostly in secret, while Hester is publicly tormented at nearly every turn. Eventually Dimmesdale dies in Hester's arms in front of a crowd of his parishioners on the same scaffold where she was pilloried at the beginning of the novel, thereby directing the reader's sympathy toward him rather than Hester.

So what does this have to do with education and grades? Inscribed in red ink across countless papers and tests, grades are scarlet letters for all to see and judge. Like the townspeople in the novel, our educational systems use grades to mark students, to label them in ways that have lasting negative effects.

The image also brings with it notions of punishment and marginalization and shame, particularly for anyone who is not a white man. Hawthorne's scarlet letter is tied to society's policing and condemnation of Hester's womanhood and sexuality, and this should not be forgotten. But at the same time, I think we can extend the metaphor more broadly to encompass the many ways that grades act as devices of regulation, surveillance, and judgment, especially for those students from historically marginalized groups. Grades are tools of injustice, and they often mirror or magnify inequities that are part of American society generally and our educational systems specifically.

At this point I would not blame you if you were thinking to yourself that I doth protest too much, to quote the Bard. You might have made it through your time in school not only having been graded but, like me, also benefiting from the privilege and status that getting good grades can afford you. Why should we subvert the status quo when it seems to work fine enough as it is? The problem is that it's not actually going fine at all, and it is much less fine for some students than for others.

But how might we go about this work? It would be impossible to target any one aspect of grades as the root cause of all the problems, because the issue is so multifaceted. Similarly, there is no single cure that will remedy our systemic ailment, because different strategies are likely to work at different levels. Rather than One Solution to Rule Them All, then, we are looking for complementary approaches that will address grades from a variety of angles. For example, there may be some overlap between the methods parents and teachers might use to help children reexamine the place of grades in their lives, but the actual technique a teacher uses to give a student feedback on schoolwork will be distinct from the messages parents will give to their kids about how to persevere when they receive negative evaluations. Efforts by both parties, however, will help children to realign their orientation to grades.

In order to take this kind of wide-angle perspective on the subject, I will dig deeply into academic research on grades, but I will also explore the human dimensions of the issue by interviewing parents, teachers, administrators, and even some students themselves. The findings of researchers in fields like psychology, sociology, and education have been crucial in shaping our understanding about the effect of grades on learning, well-being, and structural inequities, but we also need to account for the lived experience of those who have struggled with the impact of grades on their lives. In their lab research, social scientists describe human behavior using specific terminology such as causation and correlation, and they also use precisely defined, data-informed criteria to determine what can be classified using those same terms. They do so for important reasons, and we have learned much about our world and our interactions with other people because of this approach. We must also note, though, that the emotions of an individual student who is staring at a report card with low grades might defy any attempts at neat categorization. Honoring these two types of knowledge is very important to me and to the purpose of this book. What we see when we choose this combined approach is a clear, insistent message that the costs of grades far exceed any of their imagined benefits.

At the end of Hawthorne's novel, he denies his readers hope that lasting change is likely: although Hester is able to reclaim some of the symbol's power for herself by making the choice to wear it toward the end of her life, her tombstone is engraved with an A, thereby guaranteeing that her name and her legacy will forever be linked to the scarlet letter. Here is where the story of grades and our ability to make progress could, in fact, deviate from the plot of the novel. Educational transformation may yet be possible, but we will need to brave the wilderness of grades to understand how we can make it happen.

This book is intended to be unsparingly honest in outlining the problems with grades and unfailingly hopeful that we can make positive, sustainable changes in our families, schools, and colleges. I will pull back the curtain to show the damage grades can do, but I also provide a road map for altering our course. One thing is clear: children and young adults need our help, and it is within our power to make our educational institutions work for them instead of against them.

Acknowledgments

So many people contributed to the development of this book, and I am very grateful for their advice and insight.

John Warner, Giles Anderson, and Kate Adams all helped me tremendously as I was working on the original idea and, later, the book proposal. Their influence and discernment allowed me to launch this project successfully. Derek Krissoff believed in this book at a key moment, and I appreciate his advocacy for my work.

The ever-amazing librarians at the University of Mississippi never failed to respond to my many requests for interlibrary loans.

I have benefited from being part of an extraordinarily rich community of colleagues who have devoted their careers to understanding the complex world of education, and I have learned much from them about students, teaching, and the structural issues that affect our schools and colleges. I am especially indebted to Joel Amidon, Spencer Bagley, Betsy Barre, Lee Skallerup Bessette, Susan D. Blum, Tom Brady, Derek Bruff, Sarah Rose Cavanagh, Laurie Cella, Matthew Cella, Arthur Chiaravalli, David Clark, Nick Covington, Cate Denial, Jim Donahue, EJ Edney, Jennie-Rebecca Falcetta, Chris Fee, Kevin Gannon, Angela Green, Regan Gurung, Kelly Hogan, Kate Kellum, Ania Kowalik, Anindya Kundu, Jim Lang, Drew Lewis, Lindsay Masland, Katie Mattaini, Libby McFalls, Mike McFalls, Cameron Hunt McNabb, Shawnboda Mead, Heather Miceli, Ann

Monroe, Stephen Monroe, Liz Norell, Kate Owens, Robin Paige, Ian Petrie, Starr Sackstein, Viji Sathy, Allison Singley, Sue Ann Skipworth, Courtney Sobers, Rissa Sorensen-Unruh, Beth Spencer, Jesse Stommel, Robert Talbert, Eden Tanner, JT Thomas, Thomas Tobin, Megan Von Bergen, Marc Watkins, Brooke White, Todd Zakrajsek, and to audience members at the colleges and universities where I presented the ideas found within these pages during workshops and lectures. Jamie Brickhouse helped me set up many of those events, and I'm thankful for his work as well.

It has been a true privilege to work with Greg Britton at Johns Hopkins University Press. His wisdom and guidance certainly improved this book, but his support of the project has been unmatched. I am also thankful for the work of the editorial and marketing staff at the press, as well as the two anonymous readers whose comments helped make the book better.

My colleagues in the School of Education, and especially the Department of Teacher Education, at the University of Mississippi have welcomed me with open arms, and I am very grateful to them.

I interviewed many educators, parents, and students for this book. Some of those interviews made the final cut, and some did not, but I want to thank all of those who shared their stories with me.

Across the years, my students at Columbus State University, George Mason University, Rice University, and now the University of Mississippi have taught me a great deal and have opened my eyes to the obstacles that so many learners face as they seek to further their education.

I had many conversations about this book with my longtime friend and colleague Bob Cummings, and he continually blocked for me as I tried to carve out time to write in the midst of a pandemic.

Emily Pitts Donahoe, my phenomenal colleague in the Center for Excellence in Teaching and Learning at UM, read a draft of the manuscript and gave me excellent feedback.

Will Eggers, Marcus Gobrecht, Keith Hoffman, Frank Napolitano, Joshua Redding, Andy Rumbaugh, and John Sexton have served as sources of encouragement and guidance, both personally and professionally, for many years.

Andrew and Wendy Pfrenger have graced me with their friendship for more than two decades, and they have now welcomed my wife and daughter into the fold as well. They and their family have provided a respite in the form of dinners, game nights, and moments of laughter during the last few years that helped make this book a more manageable feat. They are both excellent teachers, too, and their influence is evident throughout these pages.

My extended family, especially Stephanie Fuqua, has always cheered me on as I've gone about this work.

When I was a kid, my parents—Betsy and Rick Eyler—told me that it didn't matter to them what grades I got in school as long as I worked hard and tried my best. Such a small thing made a huge difference for me. Thank you, Mom and Dad, for everything.

My daughter, Lucy, makes several cameo appearances in this book. She also served as a research assistant during some summer days when she was too bored to do anything else. In many ways, of course, the journey she takes through our educational systems must be her own, but it is her bright light and her optimism and her love of learning that inspires me to do what I can to help make things even just a bit better for her and for students everywhere. She makes me so very proud, and it is a great joy to be her dad.

And finally, my wife, Kariann Fuqua, has stood by my side through the peaks and valleys that accompany any major project—work that she understands all too well as an artist herself. It is a rare thing to have the good fortune to spend your life with someone you admire so profoundly, respect so completely, and whose judgment you trust so intuitively. It is rarer still for that person to find in your ideas the potential you yourself cannot yet see and to sharpen them considerably with her wisdom. In my marriage to Kariann, I have all of those things and infinitely more. Due simply to the privilege of traveling the same journey with her, I am a better writer and a better person. Gratitude is not nearly enough, but it is what I have.

Failing Our Future

Introduction

What Is a Grade?
And Other Important Questions

> I know you don't think they're good. But I just want to see how I did.
>
> —Lucy Eyler, at age 8, reflecting on grades

What Is a Grade?

On the surface, a grade is simply a letter, number, or mark (think check-pluses and smiley faces) given by a teacher for the purpose of conveying information to students about their work. That sounds innocent enough, right? How much damage could a single letter do, after all? And far be it from me to cast aspersions on smiley faces.

Once a student begins to receive grades, though, these marks take on a life of their own. They pile up quickly, like blocks in the old video game *Tetris*, and reach a level of magnitude that extends far beyond the degree to which a person is learning a particular subject. Schools and colleges use grades to rank and sort, categorizing and recategorizing students to the point where competition seems to matter more than education. Perhaps most significantly, grades appear on report cards and transcripts that hold a great deal of weight in determining a student's future.

Even at their most basic, grades work in contradictory ways. Sometimes they are used for the purpose of evaluation, and sometimes they are meant to function more as tools for assessment, which is a term we often see in conversations about teaching. Distinguishing between evaluation and assessment is the key, then, and the difference comes down to those old classics *intent* and *effect*. I had a creative writing professor in college who was always asking us whether the intent of our writing was ultimately married to the effect on the reader. We can use this same logic to think about grades. Is the intent of giving the mark married to the effect on the student?

When the letters, numbers, and symbols given out in schools and colleges are intended as a means of evaluating performance, they are used to make a judgment about a student's work.[1] These judgments can range from "that is only a partially correct answer" to "this essay needs more development" to "I have not seen enough evidence to promote this student to the next level." In this sense, evaluation is the primary function of grades in American educational institutions. But evaluation implies measurement and measurement implies objectivity, and—as we will see in chapter 1—grades are not objective measurements.

The effect of evaluation, and its related judgment, on the students who receive the grades is extraordinarily varied. This is understandable. Because students rarely have the opportunity to appeal their grades or redo assignments, many of these judgments are final, and they have the capacity either to open or close down so many opportunities for children and young adults. We all respond to these kinds of judgments differently, and some care very little. Others, though, take them very personally. Many equate their grades with their worth as human beings.[2] Surely, this is not what educators intend when they give grades, but it is the effect nonetheless.

When grades are used for assessment, on the other hand, it means that their primary role is to communicate feedback. We give feedback to help students grow and make progress. Feedback is rarely used to judge but is instead something like a north star meant to guide them toward a goal. Providing students with feedback—via written comments, marks like a check-plus, or even just a friendly "keep up the hard work"—is an act of care that conveys our commitment to helping them succeed. Even if students are not necessarily thrilled with the feedback they receive, they usually recognize that it represents an attempt to help them learn more and improve.

The truth, though, is that grades are rarely used for the purpose of giving feedback, and because they are so often associated with evaluation, any feedback conveyed by grades tends to be negative. Assessment and feedback happen through lots of other means in classrooms across the country, while grades tend to be reserved for judgment.

In other words, it's all very complicated, and just talking about the mark, the letter, the grade itself does not really do justice to the complexity of the issues at hand. Instead, you will be reading in the pages ahead about what I call grading models. A grading model includes the rationale and means by which a letter or a number is given as a grade, the role of feedback in the learning process, the function of student reflection in this system, and the ways in which all of these component parts are tied to an individual instructor's philosophy about education and teaching. For example, so far we have primarily been discussing traditional grading models, which are the predominant means of evaluation in American schools and colleges. In a traditional grading model, the grade itself—that is, the evaluation of a specific performance by a student on an exam, essay, or other kind of assignment—takes center stage. The feedback students receive in traditional models can certainly be helpful, but much of it is also used to justify the grade given by the teacher. In addition, very few students are ever asked to reflect on their learning or on the feedback provided by their instructors in these kinds of models.

But the cause is not yet lost. There are other kinds of grading models currently in use, either by individual instructors or entire institutions. Collectively they are sometimes called alternative grading strategies, progressive grading models, or even liberatory models. I will show you many examples of these kinds of models in the latter part of the book, but—on the surface—all of them seek to decentralize grades as a means of evaluation and to focus more on growth and improvement. They do so by prioritizing feedback, reflection, and multiple attempts at meeting learning goals. Underneath all of these newer models, however, is an explicit attempt to undo the damage wrought by our current grading systems.

How Long Have Grades Been Around?

Grades have been problematic since their beginnings. Pick up any book about grades and you are likely to see more or less the same narrative about their history in America. Ezra Stiles, the president of Yale in the late 1700s, typically receives the credit or the blame (depending on your perspective) for initiating a systematic ranking method for the students he was examining. He divided these students into four categories of performance, described in Latin, that ranged from "best" to "worse" (but luckily not "worst").[3] Stiles was clearly a guy who did not mince words.

At most, Stiles can probably be credited with popularizing for American educational institutions a British system that had been in use for a while.[4] What I think is important to emphasize about the early history of grades is that they were used solely for ranking students within groups and categorizing their performance on examinations that took place about once a year. It is also worth noting that we have never entirely moved away from this philosophy of ranking in our schools and colleges.

Naming a valedictorian and conferring Latin honors (*cum laude,* etc.) are both legacies of grading's original sin.

The letter grades with which we are more familiar arrived in America at the tail-end of the nineteenth century and then really caught fire in the twentieth century, becoming widespread in school districts and universities across the country by the 1940s.[5] Despite the momentum that led to its nearly universal adoption, though, the A–F grading system was not embraced because teachers all agreed it was the best way to measure learning. It was simply thought to be an easy, standardized way for educational institutions to communicate with each other about student performance.

Once established, letter grades proved to be so popular that the meat-packing industry developed a similar system for examining the quality of meat, though some in the field debated whether or not letters were sufficient to capture the complexities of inspecting animal flesh.[6] Educators, however, did not seem to have the same kind of qualms about continuing the use of grades to evaluate student learning.

To be honest, if we really want to understand how we can alter our current predicament with grades, then a rigid point-by-point chronology of the history of grading is much less useful than an assessment of crucial moments where we can see the wheels of progress turning. And one such moment provides us with insight into both the possibility of change and the obstacles set up before us.

The hero of this vignette is a fellow named Horace Mann. Mann sometimes makes cameo appearances in American history classes, but he's often overlooked by textbooks entirely, which is a shame given his extraordinary life. Born in 1796, he was one of the most important educational reformers and politicians of the nineteenth century. Before he died in 1859, Mann—from his home base of Massachusetts—had engineered many of the features that now define public education in America, from the tax structure that provides for local school districts to the creation of school libraries to an emphasis on continual professional development for teachers and so much more. He also thought standardized tests were a good idea, so I don't want to give you the impression that everything he did was a home run.

He served as the secretary of the Massachusetts Board of Education from 1837 to 1848 and, as part of his duties in this role, he would present a comprehensive report each year on the state's schools and curriculum. In his *Ninth Report*, published in 1846, Mann spends considerable time reflecting on the use of what he calls "emulation" as a motivator in schools. Some readers of Mann's report interpret emulation solely to mean competition—that is, students are trying to emulate their more successful peers so that they can perform better and, thus, be ranked higher in the class.[7] While he certainly did not support the overly competitive nature of the ranking system, Mann seems concerned about emulation not only because it increases competition but also because students would lose sight of their individual achievements, which he believed to be the more important outcome of education. If, he asks in the report, a student

> compares himself with himself, which may be called self-emulation,— and asks whether he knows more to-day than he did yesterday, or has acquired more during the current term of year, than he did during the corresponding part of the last term or year; if he has some elevated object before him, which he desires to reach, and rejoices in his progress towards it; all this seems not only lawful but laudable.[8]

Mann makes a substantial break here from the norms of the day by daring to suggest that individual performance may be more important than categorizing students into groups. He notes several times in this same report that others will disagree with him about emulation and that he is taking a controversial position, which illustrates the degree to which he knew he was diverging from commonly held beliefs about the purpose of schools.

Mann addresses the subject of emulation with some frequency throughout his body of work,[9] but his thoughts about emulation alone would not represent the beginning of a sea change if he had not also been obsessed with record-keeping. In his *Tenth Report*, Mann suggests that every school in Massachusetts should keep an individual report on file for each student. He referred to this document as a "register," and teachers were required to record a wealth of information about students, including their parents' names, minute details about their attendance, what they were studying, and remarks about their progress. Most of the explanatory text connected with the sample register in the *Tenth Report* has to do with the different marks teachers should use to indicate absences or tardiness and how to calculate overall school attendance.[10]

In time, the combination of this interest in the individual performance of a student and the desire to have an official account of student information would lead first to what were called deportment cards (which focused primarily on student behavior and secondarily on performance) and then later to report cards as we know them today.[11] As a result of this shift, students began to have the opportunity to see their growth over time and to make changes along the way. I really cannot overstate how revolutionary it was to move to a system where grades were envisioned as a way to provide information about an individual student's performance rather than as a tool used exclusively for comparing students to each other. While a handful of educators in Mann's time were interested in sending progress reports home to parents, it is his emphasis on the individual that sets him apart.[12] The idea that grades could be used in this way would have been entirely foreign to Mann's contemporaries. Although it took many others in addition to Mann to move education more permanently in this direction, he does deserve some credit for leading the charge here.

The push that eventually led to viewing grades as signifiers of individual progress is exciting to me, but not because I necessarily agree with the use of grades for that purpose or any purpose, really. What I think this moment in history demonstrates for us is that there is potential for change even with ideas that are firmly entrenched in our most inertia-bound institutions. If this level of transformation was once possible, then it can be possible again, although the amount of time it takes can be daunting at first. Decades passed before the transition was made from Mann's ideas to actual report cards that recorded individual grades. Like most efforts at change, the process moved in fits and starts. Incremental change is still change, though, and it is often essential to move slowly at first in order to ensure that the results are lasting. I'm just not sure we can wait much longer to reform our grading practices.

Do All Educational Institutions Give Grades?

To talk about reform with such broad brushstrokes, though, seems to suggest that every school, college, and university needs to change, but this is not necessarily the case. Montessori schools—that is, those schools that prioritize independent work and meaningful projects according to the method developed by Maria Montessori in the twentieth century—do not usually give any kind of traditional grades.[13] There are approximately 3,000 Montessori schools in America, over 500 of which are public schools of one kind or another, which means that there are a lot of students who are in schools where they are not graded.[14] Students who attend home schools often receive nontraditional evaluations as well. More to the point, there are many K–12 schools and districts that have already begun or completed the work of moving from a traditional grading model to a more progressive one, and there are even some colleges in the United States that are completely gradeless. You will hear lots more about these kinds of institutions in chapter 7, but they are still the exception rather than the rule. We need to focus on changing the many thousands of institutions that are still using the same archaic grading systems that were put in place over a hundred years ago.

Why Do We Care So Much about Grades?

We care because grades serve as gatekeepers to the many possible futures our children and young adults wish to pursue. We care because grades operate as a currency in education, and this system is rife with inequities. We care because grades are wielded as weapons and rewards. We care because grades dominate every aspect of a student's academic life. And we care because we have an astonishing amount of research showing the effect of grades on learning and on well-being. Let's take a look at some of this research now. But be ready—it's not for the faint of heart.

PART I

The Many Problems with Grades

CHAPTER 1

The Race Nobody Can Win

Grades as Obstacles
to Motivation and Learning

> Grading schemes are so characteristic of schools around
> the world that it is hard for some to even imagine a school
> without grading. Yet despite their pervasive use, there is
> remarkably little evidence that grading strategies enhance
> motivation or learning . . .
> —Richard Ryan and Edward Deci, "Intrinsic and Extrinsic Motiva-
> tion from a Self-Determination Theory Perspective," 5–6

Despite having knees that will often refuse to move the way I want them to, I sometimes run on the weekends in order to exercise and to think. I have even signed up for a 5K race or two on occasion, although I'm a permanent denizen of the back of the pack. As I trudge along the course during these events, I am aware that somewhere, far ahead of me, someone is crossing the finish line first, thereby winning the race. Unless there is a tie, which would be quite rare in a long-distance event, this process is pretty straightforward. Only one person wins, and everyone else is the not-winner. Most runners will say that they are racing only to improve their PR (which is runner-speak for personal record), and some of them are even telling the truth about this, but most would love to win even if it meant finishing with a time that was slower than they expected. When winning is a viable possibility, it is easy to run toward the reward of victory rather than focusing on our individual fitness gains. If you are like me and winning is never an option, then it becomes possible to enjoy the scenery and simply try to do better than the last time.

To some degree, this is how grades work too. They convince us that education is a race to be won rather than a process to empower children, to help them build better lives, and to pursue questions they find meaningful. Students try desperately to win the prize at all costs. But there is a key difference between grades and a weekend road race. Whereas a race has a clear winner, the "prize" of a good grade is actually a mirage. Nobody wins anything when they get a good grade. Instead, the finish line just moves back a bit further, and students are forced to run the same course over and over and over again. Rather than serving as a mark of winning, grades actually push students into a vicious loop where they just seek better and better grades, all the while missing what should be the real purpose of education—the learning that happens along the way. Grades distract from, instead of enhancing or accurately measuring, this learning.

Part of the reason for this has to do with motivation. Like ribbons for winning a race, grades are classic extrinsic motivators. The incentive to do better in a system with grades has very little to do with learning. The focus is squarely placed on the number appearing at the top of an exam or the letter recorded on a report card. Students become what Ken Bain and others have called "strategic learners," and they do only what they have to do to get the grade they need to move to the next test, the next class, or the next phase of their lives.[1] Classrooms at all levels therefore become environments where this kind of motivational framework competes significantly with the intrinsic motivation that we hope will be cultivated by our educational institutions. We want kids, teens, and young adults to learn for the sake of learning or because they are intrigued by a subject, not because they feel as if they are required to do so.

That's a rough sketch of the situation anyway. A holistic picture of motivation—particularly as it relates to grades—is a bit more complex, however.

The Messy Reality of Motivation

Researchers have been trying to understand why people do the things they do for a very long time, and although we know more about motivation than we ever have before, we still have a lot of questions remaining about what makes us tick. It's so challenging to figure out because every individual is motivated by a host of different factors, even within the course of a single day, so we can really only study a piece or two of the puzzle at any given time rather than the whole picture. Here's what we do know: in certain prescribed conditions, and for some purposes, extrinsic motivators do push people to take action, but their effectiveness derives from a coercion that is rooted in what we call behaviorism. In his highly regarded book on grades and other kinds of extrinsic motivators, *Punished by Rewards*, Alfie Kohn argues that society uses incentives like these to reinforce behaviors that are perceived to be desirable, as if we were lab animals in cages or boxes.[2]

Like these rats and cats, humans can be rather easily conditioned by rewards to comply with the needs or the wishes of others. For this reason, extrinsic motivators are particularly useful when we are asked to do things that don't really appeal to us or when compliance is the goal.[3] We go to our jobs, ultimately, because we are being paid to do so, and we might try to perform optimally if a raise or a promotion is possible, but that does not necessarily mean that we find the work itself to be personally meaningful. Similarly, students most often attend school and participate and turn in their work on time in order to get a good grade, not because they are eager to do these things. All of us are coaxed into compliance in a large number of different contexts because of the reward, the extrinsic motivator, at play.

Intrinsic motivation operates quite differently. People are more naturally driven to do things when they care about them and are genuinely interested in them. This does not mean that it is easy to be intrinsically motivated or that people in environments without extrinsic motivators magically become intrinsically motivated. It just means that when we are intrinsically motivated we are driven from within and for no expected reward other than our own enjoyment and betterment. Edward Deci, one of the world's leading scholars of motivation, describes intrinsic motivation as "*self*-motivation."[4]

Whereas extrinsic motivators are useful as incentives to get things done, intrinsic motivation is vital when we are concerned about the quality of a product, process, or performance.[5] This is the difference between just finishing a project to meet a deadline and wanting to do your best on the same project because the work matters to you. These characteristics are central to the research on grades.

In 1986, Ruth Butler and Mordecai Nisan published what is still one of the most influential papers on the subject of grades and motivation. They were interested in learning about the effect of feedback and grades on the intrinsic motivation of 261 sixth-graders. They divided the students into three groups and gave them a series of assignments to complete, and then students in the first group were given only written feedback on the assignments, students in the second group received only a grade, and students in the third group got neither a grade nor feedback.[6] What they found when they examined the results has shaped the way we have understood grades for decades.

Students in the feedback-only group not only "expressed greater interest in the tasks than did those in the other two groups," but they also were the most likely to attribute this heightened intrinsic motivation as being the source for the effort they put into the tasks and for the level of success they achieved for their performance.[7] This finding is intriguing enough, but Butler and Nisan went even further: "Our results suggest, as some critics argue, that the information routinely given in schools—that is, grades—may encourage an emphasis on quantitative aspects of learning, depress creativity, foster fear of failure, and undermine interest. They also suggest that no such negative results ensue from the use of task-related individualized comments."[8] This, I think, qualifies as the academic equivalent of a mic drop.

It is probably fair to say that nobody involved in education wants students to experience anything like this frightening laundry list of effects. Most consistent with what we have been discussing in this chapter, though, is the finding that grades, when used as the sole means of evaluation, have a negative impact on intrinsic motivation. Feedback, not grades, is the driver of intrinsic motivation, since it is nonthreatening and typically focused on individual improvement. The fact that grades also dampen our students' ability to be creative and increase their anxiety about failure further diminishes the role grades should be playing in our learning environments.

In 2021, Alison Koenka and her collaborators published an important meta-analysis (a paper that analyzes various studies on a particular topic) that reinforces what Butler and Nisan said all those years ago. They found that students who get grades perform better on educational activities than students who receive no information about their performance at all, but graded students also display "less motivation to engage in academic tasks for internal reasons and greater motivation to do so as a means to an end."[9] Even more significantly, "students who were given comments rather than solely a grade on assessments experienced heightened internal motivation and lower external motivation. These optimal patterns of motivation appeared to translate as expected into favourable learning outcomes . . ."[10] Feedback again wins the day, and we should be focusing on enhancing our use of feedback if we want students to develop more intrinsic motivation with respect to their academic pursuits.

But wait, there's more! In addition to their damaging effect on intrinsic motivation, the extrinsic aspect of grades also causes students to adopt "performance-avoidant" goals with respect to their academic work.[11] Those who take a performance-avoidant approach are trying to avoid being the worst in the class or being seen as incompetent rather than striving to be the best.[12] We see performance-avoidant goals at work when we hear things in the classroom like "How many points do I need to just get a B–?" or "What do I have to do to squeak by with a C?" As a teacher, I have often heard variants of those phrases, and it is always disheartening. Grades ultimately encourage many students only to jump through hoops, not to excel.

If we really want to understand the complexity of grades, though, we need to drill down even deeper, because the simple binary of extrinsic versus intrinsic is really not robust enough to explain the many facets of motivation. One current model for understanding motivation, called self-determination theory, suggests that extrinsic motivation is actually a broad umbrella under which sit several subgroups of motivators, some of which may lead to intrinsic motivation if they are internalized and help a person move toward developing autonomy. Last winter, for example, I participated with my family in a jigsaw puzzle competition. My wife and daughter love puzzles, and they are amazingly good at putting them together, but I have always been less enthused about the pastime. I'm not what you might call extraordinarily observant, so finding the right pieces is often just an exercise in frustration for me. They were excited about the competition, however, and I wanted to help them win the prize, so off we went. Once the contest began, I was assigned the role of putting the edge pieces together (the easiest of all jobs), and re-signedly began to collect what pieces I could find. But, to my surprise, things started to click pretty quickly, and I was enjoying the process. I wasn't doing it solely to help them win a prize anymore, but because I really was invested in completing the entire edge of the puzzle.

Sadly, we came in fourth overall in the competition, but the whole situation is a good example of the kind of motivator that has an extrinsic origin and is then internalized to the point where it is moving toward intrinsic motivation.[13] Given this kind of complicated interplay, it is possible to see why research about the effects of extrinsic motivation on intrinsic motivation has complex results.

Despite the purely extrinsic nature of grades, the more nuanced explanation provided by self-determination theory helps us to understand those who develop an enjoyment and even a passion for academic subjects in school even though they are being graded. For these folks, grades may be the initial reason to do the work and to take it seriously, but those factors become internalized and important to them despite the fact that they are still operating within a system where they are receiving grades. Crucially, this does not change the fundamental attributes of grades as extrinsic motivators, and many, many students never reach the point where they are able to find the intrinsic benefits of subjects within an extrinsic system. For these students, grades maintain their role as the primary incentives, and the detrimental effects of the system continue for them unabated.

We see the same kind of internalization with those who describe themselves as being motivated by grades in a positive way. I interviewed noted author and psychologist Sarah Rose Cavanagh for a podcast called *Tea for Teaching*, and she shared with me a compelling story about the role grades played in her life when she was in college.[14] Cavanagh explained that grades helped her to work through some of her "personal struggles with anxiety," much of which centered on social interactions. "I was anxious," she told me, "for social reasons. I was anxious about [class] participation, and I had a really hard time participating." But when she enrolled in some women's studies classes, where participation made up a significant part of the grade, she faced a dilemma: participate or risk damage to her stellar grade point average (GPA). This was enough to spur her toward making contributions to class discussion—though critically, she notes that it was the combination of this challenge alongside the context of the unusually inclusive, warm, and student-centered classes that was so transformative. In Cavanagh's case, the "grade was actually the motivator that helped me not just with my intellectual journey but also my mental health journey . . . For me, personally, grades were fun and they were also this motivator that had this huge effect on my life."

In Cavanagh's story, too, grades get the ball rolling, but the internalization of working through anxiety and contributing to the class move the motivation more toward intrinsic than extrinsic, because they helped to foster a sense of autonomy. It's a spectrum, a sliding scale. Not everyone is able to internalize to this degree, though, so it's essential that we continue to interrogate how grades operate within these motivational frameworks.

Cheating and Motivation

One final issue related to grades and motivation that we have to address is cheating. Unsurprisingly, when we place outsized emphasis on grades in our schools and colleges, we create an environment that incentivizes cheating.[15] The classroom becomes a pressure-cooker where all of the emphasis is placed on the reward, and so we send the message that getting that reward, regardless of the means, is the most important thing. Students feel this stress acutely, and some resort to cheating as a result.[16] I certainly do not condone academic dishonesty, but we must at least acknowledge that students are trapped in a system where the incentive structure is wildly misaligned with learning.

I also don't want to overstate the problem. Anecdotal estimates about the amount of cheating that is happening in classrooms are often wildly inflated, whereas we have evidence that students may in fact be cheating less than they have in the past.[17] The advent of generative AI may have an impact on these numbers, but I am also concerned with the moral panic about cheating that occurs every time a new technology enters the scene. I think education is at its best when we assume the best of students and when we trust them. The vast majority want to learn and simply seek to improve their lives, and this doesn't change just because a technology is introduced that could potentially, but not automatically, be used to cheat.

I spoke to Neil, a sophomore at a high school in Pennsylvania, about some of these issues. He described to me what he refers to as the "toxicity" of the culture at his school when it comes to grades.[18] Everyone in Neil's school talks about grades all the time, and he doesn't feel like he or his friends can ever escape their long shadow. He expressed concern at the high degree of competition caused by grades. The pressure is so intense, he told me, that honors students will sometimes decide to cheat, particularly in group texts on Snapchat, where the evidence of answer-sharing quickly disappears. Shockingly, the teachers of Neil's honors classes know that cheating is happening, and they try to stop it by suggesting that the behavior will simply help the recipients of the answers get better grades, thereby placing the person giving the answers at a competitive disadvantage. He emphasized that no one ever discusses the ethical quandary of cheating in these situations. Neil's story is not unique, but it is noteworthy for detailing the tricky messages students receive about grades and the grade-related stress that will sometimes compel them to cheat.

The Effect of Grades on Learning

If students are somehow able to find a way through this motivational morass and actually begin the process of learning, they quickly run into another set of roadblocks. Unfortunately, grades also inhibit our ability to learn in a variety of ways.

Consider for a moment something you are good at. It can be anything—tennis, crocheting, cooking, gardening, even trapeze artistry. No judgment here. Now cast your mind back and think about how you developed your skills in this area. It is likely that your mastery was the result of trying out a technique or a move or a serve, making a mistake, getting some feedback from a coach or another kind of accomplished practitioner, then trying again and starting the process all over again. This is the natural cycle of learning. Learning is iterative, and it requires failing, feedback, and multiple attempts. If I were a betting man, I would guess that you were not graded on any part of this cycle as you became more proficient. Am I correct?

Grades interrupt that cycle at every step. First, they penalize the trying. Trying something new is not an easy thing to do. It requires some degree of vulnerability, a willingness to take intellectual risks, and a level of comfort with not getting something right on the first attempt. Students are often graded on the tries, though. They are often not given much chance to practice in low-stakes, non-evaluative settings. So they learn to toe the line, to stay in their comfort zone, and not to risk too much because of the consequences for doing so. Our grading systems do not typically make possible the kind of trial and error that is necessary for learning. We send our children to school to develop the ideas that will change the world, but they come back cowed by grades into coloring only within the lines.

Grades also stigmatize failure, which is a catalyst for learning and is the expected result of trying something new for the first time. Our brains are actually built to make errors and to allocate cognitive resources in order to learn from these mistakes.[19] It would make sense, then, for schools to allow for as much of this kind of activity as possible, but grades make this nearly impossible. Grades cause failure to be considered anathema in education, and thus students are asked to work counter to the way learning happens at a biological level. Failure is regarded as something to be avoided entirely in academic work and students who fail are often cordoned off for remediation. Although some teachers are experimenting with strategies that provide students with the chance to fail within a safe, equity-minded framework in order to enhance learning, the negative associations with failure largely remain.[20]

This kind of interference is significant. The process of learning is not easy to begin with, and grades make it even more difficult by hindering the steps that are necessary to help students develop better understanding and advance their knowledge of complex subjects.

The Measurement Fallacy

There is a long-standing and damaging mythology that hangs over education like a wet blanket. It goes something like this: we cannot know if students have learned anything if they are not given grades. We simply have to dismantle this false notion. Grades are not necessary to certify that learning has taken place. We can communicate that a student has learned something by conveying that to them through feedback in one form or another, and we can share this same information with colleges, graduate schools, and future employers using feedback as well. There is nothing about a grade in and of itself that makes it better at delivering information about learning than written, spoken, or visual feedback, and—in fact—grades might be much worse tools for this due to what I call the measurement fallacy.

Despite all of what you have read over the course of this chapter, our educational systems cling to grades because they offer the supposed confidence that comes with measurement. Grades offer an illusion of scientific measurement that has proven useful for a variety of purposes. Regrettably, however, grades have never measured what we have been told they measure, and our children and young adults have paid the price.

In a 2014 paper, Corbin Campbell and Alberto Cabrera found evidence that there may not be a clear connection between grades and learning. Specifically, they conclude that "deep learning is not a necessary condition for a high GPA."[21] This is significant for a couple of different reasons. First, it means that a student who gets good grades may have learned the material well or they may not have done so. You may be asking yourself how that could be possible. I admit that it is counterintuitive, but if students are graded on effort or on noncognitive factors like attendance, teamwork, etc., then it is conceivable that they could have high grades without truly learning. The same is true if the grades for exams and papers are based in part on rote memorization or grammar, then it is also relatively easy to get a good grade without demonstrating that they genuinely understand the subject.

On the other hand, this disconnect between learning and GPA also potentially means that someone could get a low grade but could still have learned deeply. We would need more research to support this claim, but it is certainly within the realm of possibility. Students can have bad days or they may be asked to complete an assignment that does not allow them to fully demonstrate their knowledge. They may study information that does not appear on the exam. I am speculating at this point, but there are a handful of scenarios where a student could have learned deeply and still received a low grade.

Going even further, an all-star team of influential scholars joined forces in 2016 to publish one of the most important papers on grades that we have in the literature. They exhaustively analyzed a hundred years' worth of research and then conclude with this bolt of lightning:

> Grades, therefore, must be considered multidimensional measures that reflect mostly achievement of classroom learning intentions and also, to a lesser degree, students' efforts at getting there. Grades are not unidimensional measures of pure achievement, as has been assumed in the past or recommended in the present. Although measurement experts and professional developers may wish grades were unadulterated measures of what students have learned and are able to do, strong evidence indicates that they are not.[22]

That last sentence is self-explanatory, but I think the first part needs some clearing up. A "classroom learning intention" is a goal set by the instructor. If I am teaching a writing class, for example, I may want my students to craft effective introductions or produce persuasive arguments. These are my learning intentions, and I would evaluate students based on how much progress they make with respect to these targets. My understanding of their progress is based on my assessment of their work as a professional in the field, but it does not mean that other educators would judge students' progress in the same way or even have the same learning intentions to begin with.

Thus, there is no single standard when it comes to learning, and so grades cannot communicate something universal, because no such thing exists. Grades rely on criteria that are almost always subjective insofar as they are determined by an individual instructor based on an assignment created by that same teacher, who brings to the process her or his own values, beliefs about error and feedback, perspectives on the role of a teacher in helping students to learn, and a host of other factors. To be sure, the judgments made by K–12 teachers and college faculty when they evaluate work are expert judgments, but this does not change the inherent subjectivity of the determinations they make. A grade is best viewed, then, as an individual's evaluation of student work in a particular context at a particular time—nothing more, nothing less. Most importantly, grades should never be seen as incontestable data that are somehow ideologically pristine.

In fact, mathematician Sunil Singh recently declared that grades were "statistically useless," because they do not convey meaningful information and there is too much of what social scientists refer to as "noise" for them to be trusted.[23] And in a large-scale admission of defeat, the University of Michigan unilaterally decreed that some undergraduates would receive As for courses in the spring of 2023 because the graduate student teaching assistants who were assigned to evaluate them were on strike due to unfair labor conditions.[24] Nobody read the final essays and exams, but all of the students were given top grades nonetheless. This is really the icing on a rather unappetizing cake, I think. Those Michigan grades have absolutely nothing to do with learning and speak only to the institutional imperative to put a letter on a transcript.

Questioning the accuracy of grades is nothing new, though. Daniel Starch and Edward Elliott wrote a series of articles in *The School Review* during the 1910s interrogating the reliability of percentage grades in English, math, and a variety of other disciplines.[25] Each of these papers makes clear its intention of putting pressure on any claims people might make about the objectivity of grading. As a reader, I find it hard not to sense a kind of desperation in their prose, a quixotic attempt on the part of Starch and Elliott to stop a storm they could see gathering on the horizon.

Because grades are not reliable instruments for evaluation, we can also call into question any claims that grade inflation is running rampant in our schools and colleges. Grade inflation—the notion that grades are artificially higher now than they have been in the past—is a phantom menace. In order to argue that grades are inflated, there would first need to be objective benchmarks for learning in a given course in every context where that course is taught and agreement across vast numbers of faculty and educational institutions as to the criteria for evaluating those benchmarks. We have already seen that this is not the case. There would then need to be consistent evaluation over time and evidence that instructors were using the shared criteria to now give better grades for the same level of performance that would have garnered lower grades in the past. No such data exist.[26]

To be sure, some studies have revealed higher grades over time at one university or another, but a single institution cannot serve as a microcosm of education as a whole. Furthermore, simply observing that such a shift has occurred does not mean anything without digging into the criteria used to give those grades and the consistency of the learning intentions of the faculty who taught the courses.[27] In fact, one such study could find no clear explanation for the historical changes to the types of grades that had been given and suggested that it might be due to the quality of the students themselves.[28] Imagine that! And yet, grade inflation remains a favorite hobbyhorse of those who decry what they imagine to be low academic standards and who want us to clutch our pearls for fear that education is not as rigorous as it used to be.[29] These kinds of arguments are specious at their core, because they rely on assumptions and cherry-picked data rather than research.

Our use of grades as supposed measurements of learning, then, needs serious scrutiny. If I were to invent a device that I said could measure widgets, but it did not actually provide useful data about the height, width, and weight of widgets (particularly at widget factories other than my own), we would all come to the conclusion that the device was a failure and we needed a new tool. So it is with grades, but we keep using them. The absurdity of this is head-spinning, and it might even be humorous except that grades can lead to considerable harms for many kids, teens, and young adults.

Beyond Academic Debate

We have just spent some time exploring the academic nature of grades. As with anything academic, there is room for reasonable disagreement about the nuance of this or that element of motivation or learning. In fact, this kind of debate is not only warranted but desirable, because it is how we further our knowledge about a subject.

Educators, too, may disagree about how much it matters that grades affect intrinsic motivation and that they cannot provide accurate measurements of learning. If students are doing what they are supposed to do, then that might matter more to some teachers and administrators than the other points I have raised here. That is certainly not a position I endorse, but it would be naïve of me not to admit that such feelings exist.

But the academic components of grades—why they are used in schools and how they function—is only a small part of the conversation we need to have about grades, and to be frank with you, it is probably the least significant piece as well. I don't mean to suggest that the logistics of grading are not important. To the contrary, this is the starting point for all of the other ills caused by grades. The long-lasting effects of grades on students' personal lives and well-being end up being far more important, though, and it is time to take a look at those as well.

CHAPTER 2

Helicopters, Lawnmowers, and Stealth Fighters

Parents and the Pressure to Get Good Grades

> In a short period of time, we've moved from childhood and early adolescence as important developmental stages in their own right to considering them a training ground for college admissions, graduate schools, and even careers. We treat our children like young adults, simultaneously acting as if they're small children in need of perpetual oversight.
>
> —Madeline Levine, *Teach Your Children Well*, 25

Like villains in horror films, grades have long afterlives. They do not simply exist within the boundaries of school and then disappear when students step outside. Far from it, in fact. Grades reach beyond the classroom walls, and their influence is perhaps most deeply felt at home, where parents try to find ways to help their kids navigate an educational system that prioritizes evaluation and judgment over self-improvement. As a result, many parents find themselves caught in the snares of grades as well, forced to reckon with their effects on children while at the same time confronting the importance given to grades by society.

Before I go any further, I want to clarify some terminology: following the lead of researchers who study families, I am using the term "parent" here and elsewhere to mean anyone in a primary caregiving role for children. This, of course, includes birth parents, adoptive parents, relatives who have taken on parenting responsibilities for the children of other members of their family, and legal guardians.[1] Those who do the hard work of parenting are parents. That's all there is to it.

And it is no secret that parents, on the whole, have become increasingly more involved in their children's lives than was common in previous generations. Education looms large in this shift. However, parents differ dramatically in their approaches to and philosophies about school and grades based on what psychologists refer to as parenting styles. The four classical parenting styles are: authoritarian, authoritative, permissive, and neglectful. Those parents who adopt an authoritarian style have strict rules with no room for compromise and tend to be emotionally distant. Authoritative parents, on the other hand, have clear expectations for their children but allow for dialogue about these expectations, and this kind of parenting is also marked by warm relationships between parents and children. Permissive parents have that warmth as well but do not have well-defined expectations for their children and are often overly accommodating. Neglectful parenting is the most damaging style, as these parents are neither present for their children emotionally nor do they provide meaningful guidance.[2]

We have also developed more colloquial categories for parenting styles. Helicoptering, for example, is an older term and describes parents who hover over their children, watching them endlessly, checking on everything even when they are not invited to do so. Lawnmower parents, on the other hand, obliterate every obstacle that sits in front of their children.[3] More recently, parents from my own generation—Gen X—have been labeled "stealth fighter" parents: we only swoop in when something rises to the level of our concern and then train all of our energies on that particular issue.[4] Guilty as charged.

Most of these parenting styles, regardless of whether they are organized into scientific or more popular categories, derive from genuine love and a desire to protect children. Often this allows kids to feel supported, but it can also lead to the problem of parental pressure. In the service of what they believe to be their children's best interests, parents will sometimes put an extraordinary amount of pressure on their children to succeed in school, on the playing field, in extracurricular activities, and elsewhere.

This is where grades come in. The emotional and psychological strain of trying to get good grades in order to live up to the expectations of others can add to or even surpass the intrinsic burden children have already placed on themselves. As Jessica Lahey, author of *The Gift of Failure*, writes: "Applying pressure in the form of control is the single most damaging thing parents and teachers can do to their children's learning."[5] Parental pressure can heighten a child's perception that grades are more important than learning, and it sends a signal, sometimes overtly, sometimes more subtly, that love and respect are somehow contingent on performance in the classroom. Although our only intention may be to help our children do well or try their hardest, the message often reads differently to the child her- or himself.

Even the best-case parenting scenarios are not immune to pressure-related issues. For example, studies have consistently shown that authoritative parenting—the style emphasizing warm connections and clear expectations—leads to better academic outcomes for students overall.[6] The consensus seems to be that by prioritizing supportiveness and encouragement, authoritative parents create a foundation for "a high level of emotional security that provides their children with a sense of comfort and independence that, in turn, helps their children succeed in school."[7] Yet, as we will see in just a moment, even parents who fully embrace this approach will often feel themselves pulled in a number of different directions and will exert some pressure about grades although they don't necessarily want to do so.

The situation is compounded by the ubiquitous presence of online grading portals in schools. The common use of these portals, where students and their parents can view their grades at any hour of the day, creates a condition where children and teenagers cannot escape scrutiny and are constantly confronted by the pressure to do better.

Those Dreaded Portals

On the long list of blights that have darkened the hallowed halls of education, grading portals are a relatively new entry. Their rise in popularity can be attributed largely to the intensified focus on data and metrics that the No Child Left Behind Act of 2002 brought with it.[8] Grading portals are pitched as a means for better communication between teachers and parents, but they operate more as a surveillance tool, leaving students struggling to flee the gaze of an academic version of Big Brother. While we do have some evidence that the use of grading portals can "help to reduce students' course failures," I wonder if there is another way to assist in these efforts that balances the objective good of decreasing the number of students who are failing with the potential costs incurred by the portals and the pressures they can bring with them.[9] When we add to this the finding that minoritized families disproportionately face issues with accessing the portals, either due to socioeconomic or language-related factors, then the burden falls on those who support portals to argue for their usefulness.[10]

One example of the power of these portals comes from Cathy, who attends an honors middle school in Virginia. At Cathy's school her teachers alert students immediately after they have posted grades to their portal. According to what Cathy's friends tell her, parents will check the site shortly after this, and kids will try to sneak a peek on their phones during class or at lunch.[11] This level of fixation is clearly problematic, and Cathy's story illustrates the viselike grip that grades have on families as well as the ways in which portals drive this dynamic.

In my own family, we have taken the advice of Lahey in *The Gift of Failure* when it comes to grading portals. We tell Lucy that we will only look at the portal if there is something she wants to show us, whether that be something she is proud of or as a way to let us know that she is concerned about a class.[12] We are willing to sacrifice the immediacy of information about her assignments so that we can release the pressure valve a bit, although we know she carries other kinds of stressors about her academic performance, particularly as the only child of two college educators.

Grading portals are just the most recent lever parents can pull to apply pressure, though. They can't take the fall for everything, but they can be blamed for some of the more intense scrutiny on children's grades. On the whole, parental pressure takes many forms and has many sources. Some parents are driven by their own achievement goals, and they transfer these to their children. Others simply want to help their kids prepare for an uncertain future, and they do not understand the unintended consequences of their actions. Still others believe that the ends (eventual success in life) justify the means (pressure). These are the tiger parents made famous by Amy Chua's book on the subject.[13] One major reason for parental pressure, though, is status—particularly the intersection between social status and class status. Parents hope their children will either gain more status than they themselves have, through the kind of upward class mobility that brings with it an enhanced potential for wealth and economic security, or they want their children to retain their family's social and class status.

Regardless of the reason for the pressure, it is damaging nonetheless—damaging to family dynamics, damaging to the relationships between parents and children, damaging to the kids themselves.[14] Let's dig a bit deeper to see why this is the case.

Achievement Goals

It is probably not a shock to you by this point to learn that parents have different kinds of goals with respect to the academic achievement of their children. Researchers tend to cluster these goals in two different categories: learning goals and performance goals. Parents who are oriented more toward performance focus primarily on the outcome—grades, awards, etc. On the other hand, parents who adopt learning goals for their children are much more likely to value the stops, starts, and meanderings that accompany any journey toward knowledge. For these parents, the emphasis is on understanding, not rewards.[15]

This is not to suggest that all parents are neatly divided into one camp or another. It is entirely possible that one person could be oriented toward a child's performance in school but embrace learning goals in sports, and vice versa. It is even possible that a parent could have performance goals tied to a specific subject in school (like math, for instance), but have learning goals for other subjects. What we do know, though, is that parental performance goals often lead to children who feel more pressure and, in some cases, to what researchers have called "dysfunctional perfectionism."[16] Girls, in particular, are more likely to feel anxious because of this kind of pressure.[17]

Beyond simply providing a framework for their approach to grades, achievement goals also drive parental behaviors related to their children's academic pursuits. Common parental behaviors related to academics include involvement in activities, monitoring progress, helping with homework, etc. Parents with learning goals, who focus on the holistic development of the child as learner, use behaviors that lead to better results all around than those who concentrate on the outcome instead of the child.[18]

As parents, we bring to our role our own academic successes and failures, and this may be part of what shapes our achievement goals for our children.[19] This is perfectly understandable, but we cannot use the past as an excuse for our behaviors in the present and the future. We need to be intentional in reflecting on the ways in which our own experiences are motivating our responses to our children. Only then can we undo some of the harmful legacy of grading for both ourselves and those we love.

Concern for the Future

Another source of parental pressure is the clash between wanting our children to be successful and happy while simultaneously facing the hard truth that our educational system uses grades as keys to possible futures that might otherwise remain locked. Parents can say all the right things, adopt styles and goals that are nurturing, and still have to confront the reality that our schools, colleges, and universities, and the vocations beyond them, are governed by an intense focus on and obsession with grades and performance. This tug-of-war can lead to parents exerting pressure on their kids, not because they are callous, but because they cannot control the uncertainty that stems from a world structured this way.

Erika, a mother of three from the Nashville area, told me that her family feels constrained by the emphasis on grades: "My kids did Reggio preschool [a child-centered type of education similar to the Montessori method], and we were at the library three times per week. I could not keep up with their curiosity. They had gifted IEPs [Individualized Educational Plans] and objectively high creativity. Now that they are in high school with all Advanced Placement (AP) classes and 4.7 GPAs, I do not think they have read a book for pleasure in a year." She went on to say that "grades and test scores are the gatekeepers to schools and degrees which lead to professions that they will find intellectually stimulating. It all feels like a trap. Sometimes I want to move to a deserted island and let them spend their entire day observing turtles."[20] While living a life devoted to turtle-watching is probably not in the cards for most of us, it is hard not to identify with Erika's frustration here. In fact, the sentiment of feeling trapped was common among many parents I spoke with. Erika made sure to emphasize that she tries her best not to pressure her kids, but the familiar scenario she describes here can often lead to that outcome.

DeeDee, a mother of two from Dallas, feels a sense of urgency as she tries to find a solution to this grading trap.[21] "Growing up in a Black family," she explained, "education was the way out of poverty and racism." This deeply ingrained principle shaped her early beliefs about the importance of grades. DeeDee and her husband also feel compelled to focus intently on grades because of the emphasis placed on academic performance by their community, church, and friends. "The system," she says, "got the better of us," and she admits to applying some pressure to her children, one of whom is now in high school and the other is in middle school. After a while, though, she saw that this pressure was having a serious effect on the kids, noting that "they were both perfectionists, and it was crippling them." She quickly added that she remembers thinking, "I've created a monster. I need to step back."

DeeDee began changing her perspective on grades, and tried to help her children do the same. She started seeing grades as "social constructs, fake ideas, irrelevant," as part of a structure designed from the outset to distract us from learning and instead force us into a situation where we are constantly chasing the next reward. This approach has worked for her son. Her daughter, on the other hand, is in high school and is striving to be valedictorian. She, DeeDee says, is "still a perfectionist, but now finds value in learning. [Grades were] almost like a religion before, but now she doesn't believe in the system."

Ultimately, DeeDee confesses, she "feels like we can't give up on grades," because of the role they play in college admissions, but she and her family have worked diligently to deemphasize them as much as they believe is reasonably possible. The hard truth for parents is that there is no easy answer to this dilemma. We care deeply for our children, and part of that care means wanting the best for their future, but because we cannot know what that future will be, we are stuck trying to control what is within our purview. For many, that means their children's academic performance, and it can contribute to a pressure-filled relationship with kids.

The stakes are high, not least because parents often want their children to be better positioned in life than they themselves are. They want their kids to have better jobs, better careers, live in better houses, and all of that requires a kind of social mobility that they see as being tied to grades. That's not necessarily an incorrect sentiment, but it's much more complicated than meets the eye.

Status and Mobility

I grew up in a very small Pennsylvania town, and I come from a family of modest means. My mom spent her entire professional life working as an administrative assistant and transcriptionist in doctors' offices and hospitals. She was surrounded by people who had much more money than she would ever make, and—understandably—came to see being a doctor as a gateway to a different kind of life. Because of this, she frequently encouraged me to pursue a career as an anesthesiologist. Now, if you have ever met me, you'll know that the thought of spending my life working with needles and making calculations about how much medicine is sufficient to put someone under but not to do permanent damage is enough to make me flee from the room in terror, which was similar to my reaction when she first presented me with this idea. Although she pushed a bit, my mom's goal here was less about dictating what she wanted me to do with my life, and much more about making sure that I would be financially secure, that I wouldn't have to struggle in the same way that she and my dad had for so long. In the end, she trusted me to make decisions about my future that would put me in a position where I would not have to worry about money as much as she always did. I have always appreciated that trust and have benefited significantly from it.

Like my mom, many parents see education as the means for their children to secure a career that will allow them to acquire a different level of socioeconomic status, and they view grades as the necessary vehicle for this particular kind of mobility.[22] There is a kernel of truth to this, of course. Recent studies, including a 2022 report from the National Center for Education Statistics, show that those who have attained a college degree are far less likely to be unemployed.[23] But the intellectual maneuvering it takes to jump from this statistic to thinking that everyone will land a job that will set them up for life is thorny, and the costs of pushing children to attain good grades in the hopes that this will happen are potentially enormous. In order to ensure this future for their children, many families are going into serious debt to pay not just for college but also for SAT/ACT preparatory classes, tutors, and other kinds of educational consultants long before the application process begins.[24] Some parents (thankfully, very few) are even resorting to criminal bribery in order to gain admission for their children to the university of their choice, as the Varsity Blues scandal in the summer of 2019 revealed.[25] That is an extreme example, but it is a telling one too.

While most of the conversation about education and status focuses on finances, it is important to note that grades are a major player here as well. Parents often believe that college admission depends on having a flawless GPA. Before they even get to the stage where they are considering how to pay for college, then, many parents are putting intense pressure on their children to get good grades so that they can target a future that enhances or improves their social or class status and their family's as well. It probably does not need saying, but thinking about education in this way does not center a child's health, well-being, or role as a learner. In fact, this entire approach sends a message to children that parents are more concerned with themselves or with the child's career prospects than they are with whether or not the child is actually successful in that career or in their life as a whole. Grades are a central, yet seldom discussed, part of this family dynamic.

Even if parents recognize that they might be exerting unreasonable pressure on their kids, it can still be difficult to change their behavior, particularly given the realities of higher education and the workforce. Still, the well-being of our children depends on breaking this cycle, and we can begin to do so by taking a step back and assessing our priorities for their futures and for our relationships with them. Are we only interested in their financial security or do we care about their happiness and having a meaningful connection with them going forward? It may be true that one approach to parenting is to get children to the point of financial independence and then to say, "Look! I did my job," but is that all we want for them? Happiness and financial stability are certainly not mutually exclusive—and, in fact, there are research-based correlations between the two—but, at the same time, economics is only one piece of the puzzle.[26] Surely, we all know folks who have high-paying jobs and are miserable in them. It's not just about finding the right job, in other words, but finding the right job *for them*.

This brings us back to college. If we shift from thinking about the college search as something that is primarily about prestige and status to one tied to our children's personal aspirations, then we can take some of the pressure off of their grades. There are two reasons for this. First, attending the most elite institutions— where competition is high, admission rates are extraordinarily low, and the emphasis on having superhuman grades is intense— is simply not necessary to fulfill the career goals that most people have. You don't have to go to Harvard to be an amazing teacher, doctor, engineer, writer, banker, entrepreneur, or chef, just to name a few professions. In fact, liberal arts colleges or public universities are often the better fit for those who are seeking these careers because they have stellar programs as well and students there get a lot of support from their mentors. Students definitely need good grades to get into these institutions, but they don't need perfect grades, and that matters.[27] To be fair, there are rare exceptions to this advice. Students who hope to be Supreme Court justices or to study ancient Arabic texts will have to think very carefully about the colleges they choose to attend, but—honestly—most people will not need to narrow down their list of potential alma maters so drastically.[28]

Second, an A in a college calculus course does not matter so much for someone who wants to be a professor in the humanities (take my word for it), in the same way that an A in American history isn't incredibly necessary for someone who wants to study science. In fact, leaders of college career centers are now reporting that employers often care less about GPA than they do about skills like problem-solving and communication.[29] Forcing perfection in all academic areas, then, just doesn't make sense. Doing so ultimately dilutes the energy that children and young adults can put into the areas where they truly excel, and the constant drive toward impeccable achievement, as William Deresiewicz has discussed, often leads even the most accomplished students to question the purpose of their education.[30]

There is a lot of irony here. The pressure that parents can put on their children to ensure a bright future often backfires in one way or another, undermining the very success that was the original goal. And it can have lasting negative consequences.

When Pressure Becomes Abuse

Parental pressure can be detrimental enough on its own, but sometimes it crosses the line into abuse. The more extreme forms of pressure, for example, are not altogether indistinguishable from the kinds of criticism and manipulation that are classified as types of emotional or psychological abuse by the US Department of Health and Human Services.[31] Even if the emotional impact does not rise to the level of official categorization as abuse, it can still affect a child in both the short and the long term.

Even more tragically, we have research showing a connection between grades and parental violence. In 2018, the highly regarded *Journal of the American Medical Association Pediatrics* issued a report that was later picked up and publicized widely by the *New York Times*. In the paper, researchers analyzed all of the verified cases of child physical abuse during a single academic year in the state of Florida. In order to be counted in their data, incidents had to be confirmed by the state's child welfare agency. All told this amounted to 1,943 incidents during the academic year. The authors found that rates of physical abuse on the Saturdays that followed the release of a report card on a

Friday were almost four times higher than those on the Saturdays that were not connected to report card distribution.[32]

These data mirror a pattern that has been observed since at least the late 1980s, when *Time Magazine* published a piece showing a connection between child abuse and the delivery of report cards.[33] Other papers published around the same time underscore the association between grades and abuse, but it is not a subject that has been explored as much as you might expect given the seriousness of the issue.[34]

One notable exception to this gap in coverage is a piece by Sara Mandell, formerly the special assistant in the Baltimore Mayor's Office for Children and Youth, who wrote an account of a program developed during the '90s in that city to address the cases of abuse that were tied to report cards. Mandell and her colleagues developed an insert they enclosed with report cards that stated: "At Report Card Time: STOP whatever you are doing, LOOK at your child's report card, LISTEN to what your child has to say. If you are happy with your child's report card, say so! If not use the tips on the other side of this card."[35] The guidelines listed on the flip-side of the insert were proactive strategies focused on specific actions a parent could take (such as calling tutoring services) to help their children improve their performance at school. The "STOP, LOOK, and LISTEN" program, as it came to be known, was paired with a public relations campaign that featured the mayor of Baltimore talking about positive parenting approaches.[36] The result of the campaign was quite telling. In 1990 there were 90 cases of documented child abuse cases related to report cards in Baltimore, whereas in 1991—the year after the program was implemented—there were only two cases.[37] I can find no evidence that the program continued in the city beyond the early part of that decade, but other cities asked to replicate the insert for their own school districts, so the legacy of "STOP, LOOK, and LISTEN" is an important one.

Obviously, these acts of child abuse are rare occurrences committed by deeply flawed adults, but the fact that they happen at all and that grades are a factor in any way should lead to an immediate reappraisal of their role in educational systems across the country.

Gardeners or Carpenters?

In a 2017 book, renowned developmental psychologist Alison Gopnik uses the twin metaphors of gardeners and carpenters to explain different approaches to parenting. Gardeners cultivate environments that provide children with what they need to flourish, while carpenters try to build the perfect child according to a plan they carry around in their minds.[38] Although no gardener can predict the outcome of a gardening season, or the shape of a child's life, the process they use and the attention they bestow are intended to give those in their care the best chance for success. Carpenters are most interested in the final outcome, and their meticulous use of tools and awareness of their materials are employed in the service of constructing a high-quality life for their children.

Gopnik goes on to write, "Even if we humans could precisely shape our children's behavior to suit our own goals and ideals, it would be counterproductive to do it. We can't know beforehand what unprecedented challenges the children of the future will face. Shaping them in our own image, or in the image of current ideals, might actually keep them from adapting to changes in the future."[39] We now know that the pressure to get good grades is part of this counterproductivity. It simply does not help children and young adults in the way that our society seems to think it will, and instead it can do real harm. Our efforts as parents could be put to far better use—more tending of the soil and less bending materials to fit a prescribed mold. Not only is this kind of care and responsiveness more helpful for our children and their learning, but it can benefit their mental health as well. And as we will see in chapter 3, attending to children's emotional and psychological well-being is crucial right now.

CHAPTER 3

The Weight of Their World

Grades and the Mental Health Crisis in America

> Every child's path to adulthood—reaching developmental
> and emotional milestones, learning healthy social skills,
> and dealing with problems—is different and difficult. Many
> face added challenges along the way, often beyond their
> control. There's no map, and the road is never straight.
>   But the challenges today's generation of young people
> face are unprecedented and uniquely hard to navigate. And
> the effect these challenges have had on their mental health
> is devastating.
>   —Dr. Vivek Murthy, Office of the US Surgeon General, *Protecting
>   Youth Mental Health: The US Surgeon General's Advisory*, 3

The epigraph for this chapter is taken from Surgeon General
Vivek Murthy's official advisory on youth mental health, which
was released by his office in December of 2021. The high visibil-
ity of the advisory allowed Murthy and his colleagues to sound
the alarm on what can only be called one of the most serious
emergencies of our time—the rapid acceleration of psychological issues in children, teenagers, and young adults. In fact, the
word "crisis" is used throughout the document to signify the
gravity of this moment for the young people in our lives. Many
are suffering, and some are even dying, in numbers that are
higher than we have ever seen.

There are, of course, numerous reasons for this crisis. It would be foolhardy, and frankly disingenuous, to assert that one cause is more prominent than others when there are so many intersecting possibilities. The same holds true for an individual's mental health. The inner worlds of human beings are remarkably complex, and a person's psychological and emotional well-being is affected by a lot of different factors. But you are reading a book about grades, and I want to share some thoughts about why grades are relevant to a discussion of the mental health epidemic we are seeing in our communities.

Because this is such an important issue, and a sensitive one as well, I want to go step by step here. First, we need to understand the role played by academic stress, including grade-related stress, in contributing to the psychological challenges experienced by adolescents and young adults. Once we make this very important link, we will zoom our camera lens out and explore the broader scope of the mental health crisis before turning our attention to the ways in which schools and colleges are responding to this national emergency.

Before we go on, you should know that we will be dealing with some tough topics here, so please take your own care seriously as well.

The Dangers of Academic Stress

The noted psychologist and writer Lisa Damour opens one of the chapters of her book *Under Pressure* with a subheading that states "School Is Supposed to Be Stressful."[1] I fundamentally disagree with her on this point. School is not inherently *supposed* to be stressful, but it often is. School is supposed to be a place of learning, discovery, friendship, even joy, but it has become more and more stressful for students because the purpose of schooling has been contorted by mandatory testing, rigidly prescribed curricula, and an overbearing emphasis on evaluation and grades. Students put an enormous amount of pressure on themselves to meet the ever-increasing demands of school, and their teachers can sometimes add to this stress both through the criteria they use to grade and also the messages they send about the perceived importance of grades. As we know from the last chapter, parents play a role in grade-related stress too.

To be clear, I am not suggesting that we abandon academic standards or that all tasks and assignments that lead to difficulty are evil. We learn from making mistakes and getting feedback on those errors, so miscues, frustration, even confusion are all important parts of developing a richer understanding of a subject. I just think we need to be careful about how we frame our goals for education. For example, social scientists differentiate between positive stress (the technical term for this is "eustress") and negative stress (or "distress") and even between "facilitating" and "debilitating" kinds of anxiety.[2] These are useful distinctions to make when doing research in labs, but I am not sure that we are tuned in to this level of nuance as we go about our daily lives. Does a student nervous about taking a test think to herself, "Is this facilitating anxiety I'm feeling right now or has it crossed over into debilitating territory?" Does a student who needs a certain grade to keep his scholarship wonder if the stress he is feeling is positive or negative? The answer to both of these artfully constructed hypotheticals is probably "no." Despite the fact that moderate amounts of stress can potentially contribute to more focused performance, students primarily experience uneasiness in these situations.[3] Simply put, due to the potentially negative consequences for mental health, the discomfort of stress should not be our target in schools and universities.

It is well documented that stress can have a detrimental effect on physical health, psychological well-being, and cognitive function.[4] This is true of all kinds of stress, including academic stress, a category in which grades play a major part. Researchers have long been calling attention to the harms of academic stress for students. In 1993, for example, the psychologist Russell Jones published an important paper in which he underscores that stress for teenagers is a "causative factor in the development of somatic, behavioral, and psychological disorders." Among the most serious effects of stress on kids in this age group include "psychosomatic illness, suicide, substance abuse, delinquent behavior, and juvenile crime. It has been suggested that these activities are symptomatic of stress and thereby, indicative of increasing stress within this age group." What Jones provides for us here is a fairly simple equation: heightened stress = serious consequences for psychological health, especially for teenagers.

Jones then follows his discussion of the impact of stress with what we might call the kicker. "A substantial proportion of the stress affecting adolescents," he notes, "is likely to originate from academic activity. This is a consequence of the considerable proportion of students' lives spent within the school environment or under the influence of academic concerns. Indeed, academic problems are known to be among the most commonly reported sources of stress for adolescents."[5] Academic stress, then, is directly related to psychological issues for students, and grades are a major piece of this complex puzzle. Grades may not be the sole cause of academic stress, and therefore the subsequent mental health challenges many teens experience, but they are undeniably a significant contributing factor.

Here's the thing, though: by my count, 1993 was approximately 30 years ago. We have known about all of this for quite a while, but we have not really moved the needle in terms of solving the problem.[6] In fact, the situation has gotten even worse in the intervening years, and the stress connected to grades begins as early as elementary school.[7] Kimberly, a mother from Rhode Island, shared with me that her 9-year-old daughter experiences a high degree of stress that is caused by what seems to be a rather opaque grading model at her school. "To arbitrarily designate grades without firm metrics," she said, "is frustrating. My child gets + and – too, and nowhere does it explain what that means." Kimberly went on to say, "My daughter is the type of personality that wants direction, constructive criticism, feedback, or corrective actions. The grading system we currently have provides no feedback for how to do better. [She] will literally melt down saying she doesn't know what she did wrong or how to do better. She gets incredibly frustrated and she will literally tell me it stresses her out as she doesn't understand how to do better." It seems improbable to me to believe that this kind of response is what the school intends by using the kind of grading model it has developed, but the effect on Kimberly's daughter is real nonetheless.[8]

As children grow older, the stress intensifies. According to a 2018 Pew Research Center survey of children aged 13–17, 96% of those who responded said that anxiety and depression are either a "major" or "minor" problem among their peers.[9] In that same survey, 88% of respondents reported that they feel "a lot" or "some" pressure to get good grades, with 61% falling into the highest category of feeling a lot of pressure. These responses were enough to put grades at the top of the list in terms of the sources of pressure felt by the teenagers who took the survey. In a distant second place to grades was the issue of personal appearance. For the sake of comparison, it is useful to see how respondents rated the pressure they feel about their appearance, with 66% saying they feel a lot or some pressure to look good, but only 29% indicating they feel a lot of pressure about this.[10] The fact that grades are ranked so highly here is a telling marker of the outsized importance they hold for teens.

The situation for college students is no better. The American College Health Association's National College Health Assess-

ment for Fall 2022 shows that academics is second only to pro-
crastination in terms of the percentage of cis men, cis women,
and trans/gender nonconforming students who said it caused
"problems or challenges" for them over the course of the previous year. Crucially, though, academics was at the top of the list
when the question shifted to asking about which of the issues
caused moderate or high distress for those who reported struggling with a particular problem.[11] For this group, grades were not
the top stressor, but they did contribute to the most acute stress
these college students felt.

Understandably, the COVID-19 pandemic has intensified
teens' academic stress related to grades as well, with propor-
tional effects on mental health issues. In a survey conducted by
Challenge Success—a nonprofit organization associated with the
Stanford Graduate School of Education—and NBC News, 56%
of high school student respondents indicated that they felt more
stressed about school than they did before the pandemic. The
top-ranked reason for this stress was "grades, tests, and other
assessments."[12] Far from being the cause of grade-related pressure, though, the pandemic has simply exacerbated a stressor
students have been struggling with for quite some time.

Even more seriously, a 2015 fact sheet from the Centers for Disease Control and Prevention spotlighted a connection between
grades and suicidal thoughts and behaviors. Specifically, the CDC
noted that high school students who received mostly Ds and Fs
were more likely than students who received mostly As to:

- Feel sad or hopeless nearly every day for at least two
  weeks in a row
- Seriously consider attempting suicide
- Make a plan about how they might attempt suicide
- Attempt suicide[13]

Even 23% of students who received mostly A grades felt sad or hopeless almost every day for two or more weeks in a row, with 14% of students receiving these top grades also seriously considering attempting suicide.

Some caveats are in order here. From the outset, it is crucial to note that any discussion of suicidal ideation or suicide attempts must be conducted responsibly so as not to further any harm for survivors or descendants. As such, I will adhere closely to established guidelines for reporting on suicide here and elsewhere in the chapter.[14] Furthermore, the CDC is very careful to note that "these associations do not prove causation," meaning that we should not see grades as the sole basis for these behaviors but instead as part of a constellation of factors contributing to psychological distress.[15] It is perhaps even more productive to see lower grades here as being just as often one of the symptoms of crisis as they are a contributor. Clearly, though, one of the preeminent health organizations in America felt the relationship between grades and these behaviors was significant enough to call our collective attention to it.

All of this matters a great deal. If we are in the midst of a mental health emergency, and we have evidence to show that academic stress and grades are contributing to the psychological issues faced by kids and young adults, then it stands to reason that we will need to address the role that grades play in this crisis if we are going to help the many who are struggling.

The Making of a Crisis

And the numbers here are truly sobering. Each year, the Substance Abuse and Mental Health Services Administration (SAMHSA), which is a part of the Department of Health and Human Services, collects data on the psychological well-being of youth 12 to 17 years old via the National Survey on Drug Use and Health (NSDUH). The survey is one of the most respected and all-encompassing tools we have available to us for understanding the mental health landscape for adolescents. According to NSDUH, over a period of 10 years (from 2007 to 2017) the number of youths in this age group who had experienced a major depressive episode increased from an estimated 2 million to 3.2 million.[16] By 2020, the last year for which we have survey data that has been fully analyzed by SAMHSA, that number had increased to roughly 4.1 million, or 17% of that population.[17] In this context, a major depressive episode refers to a serious occurrence categorized by "at least one period of 2 weeks or longer in the past year when for most of the day nearly every day, they felt depressed, or lost interest or pleasure in daily activities" as well as "problems with sleeping, eating, energy, concentration, self-worth, or having recurrent thoughts of death or recurrent suicidal ideation."[18]

Similarly, the CDC's Youth Risk Behavior Survey tracks the numbers of high school students nationwide who are struggling with their mental health as well as those who experience suicidal ideation and/or make a suicide attempt. The results of the 2021 survey, the latest one for which we have data, indicate that 42% of high school students in this country have had persistent feelings of sadness or hopelessness during the past year. That number represents a 14% increase since 2011. Regarding what the survey refers to as "suicidality," 22% reported seriously considering attempting suicide in the past year, 18% made a suicide plan, 10% attempted suicide, and 3% were injured in a suicide attempt.[19] As if all of this weren't terrible enough, the percentage of girls in each of these categories was higher than those of boys, sometimes by twice as much. The magnification of the mental health crisis for girls is corroborated by other research as well, and it means we need targeted interventions to help different groups of adolescents rather than uniform solutions across the board.[20]

The data on college students tell a very similar story. If anything, though, the transition to college actually ups the ante, so to speak, for mental health because it is a turbulent time emotionally, physically, and psychologically for young people. B. Janet Hibbs and Anthony Rostain, experts on adolescent psychology and the authors of *The Stressed Years of Their Lives: Helping Your Kid Survive and Thrive during Their College Years*, explain that

> certain disorders typically emerge right before and during the college years. Eating disorders reach their peak among young women, while binge drinking and substance abuse hit their crest among young men . . . Combine the psychological and social vulnerabilities of college-age kids with the heightened stress of leaving home and learning to swim in an academic shark tank, and it's easy to see why the core symptoms of so many mental health disorders appear at this vulnerable time in their lives.[21]

College is thus a crucible in which strain and stress from a number of different sources (note the description of academics as a "shark tank") can cause behaviors and psychological issues that were previously latent or suppressed to surface. In other words, college presses the gas pedal on the vehicle of a mental health crisis that was already proceeding swiftly.

The Healthy Minds Network, an organization led by a group of faculty from several research universities, has been exploring different aspects of college students' mental health since 2007.[22] Its report for the 2021–22 academic year includes an analysis of more than 95,000 survey responses and ultimately shows that 44% of respondents experienced major or moderate depression, with 23% having experienced major depression. Thirty-seven percent struggled with an anxiety disorder, and 15% experienced suicidal ideation.[23] A key feature of the Healthy Minds Network survey is that respondents must have filled out a validated health assessment screening tool that essentially diagnoses them with a particular condition in order for them to be officially counted in one category or another. In other words, the survey goes beyond self-reported data and uses health metrics as confirmation.[24] Doing so is a double-edged sword. On the one hand, the survey is trying to counter any potential assumptions or misunderstandings among respondents that other major research tools might open themselves up to. On the other hand, though, using these kinds of health assessments reinforces the medicalized lens through which society tends to view mental illness, which has often led in the past to marginalization of those dealing with psychological issues.

That said, the data from the Healthy Minds Network's instrument are robust and revealing. A recent paper assessing the findings from the surveys given by the network between 2013 and 2021, for example, identifies a 50% increase in the number of college student respondents during that period who "met criteria for one or more mental health problems."[25] Given that the total number of respondents for those years surpassed 350,000, this uptick is huge. Not only is progress eluding us on this front, but we are losing ground, and the stakes couldn't be higher.

The COVID-19 pandemic is certainly responsible for very recent surges in psychological and emotional needs for both younger students and those who are in college as well.[26] However, I do not want to focus much on this COVID-related spike, because the mental health emergency we are facing began before COVID, and it will be with us long after the most intense phase of the pandemic has passed. It is too easy to become complacent when we rely on the pandemic as an explanatory force for so many of society's current ills. Doing so encourages people to think, "Well, as soon as we are through with this, everything will settle down." That is exactly the kind of philosophy that is sure to sustain the crisis rather than abate it. The short-term heightening of mental health issues brought on by COVID is a piece of the problem, not the entirety of it. We therefore need to address all of the root causes, rather than directing all of our attention to the latest one.

So let's talk about how grades might tie back into this larger discussion. I don't recall much about the math classes I took as a kid, but I do remember something called the reflexive property. It goes something like this: if $a = b$ and $b = c$, then $a = c$. If we know that we are in the midst of a mental health emergency, and we also know that academic stress—especially stress related to grades—is a significant contributing factor for some of the psychological issues faced by students, then any reasonable person must admit that grades have some kind of role in our current crisis. I am not brazen enough to suggest that grades play a primary role here, but the fact that they have any part in this at all should give us pause. It is simply unforgivable, because grading is a monster of our own creation, and it demands some kind of sustained response from our educational institutions. But have they responded? And if so, how?

The K–12 Response

Because of the scope of the emergency and the attention currently being trained on it by national leaders, there can be no doubt that it is on the radar of nearly every school district in America. The most obvious way to address the increase in student needs would be to hire enough school counselors and psychologists to meet the demand, but this has not happened. As recently as the 2020–21 academic year, approximately 40% of school districts (a statistic that represented 5.4 million students at that time) did not have a school psychologist at all, and only 8% of districts had a ratio of school psychologists no larger than one per 500 students, which is a standard endorsed by the National Association of School Psychologists. Similarly, only 14% of districts had a ratio of school counselors no greater than one per 250 students, which is the guidance set forth by the American School Counselor Association.[27]

There are several reasons for this shortage, but the most important of them has to do with resources. How a school district responds to the mental health crisis is tied directly to its resources—both financial and human—and many such resources are and have always been limited. The hiring pool for school psychologists and counselors has not been deep even in the best of times, so many schools either have lengthy wait lists for students who need to see school staff or they are forced to outsource their students to local health care providers or both.[28] Some districts are even contracting with companies that deliver telehealth services in order to expand the avenues by which students can get the help they need.[29]

Another way that schools can support students is related to the curriculum. There has been a recent push for districts to teach about mental health and, more specifically, to share strategies that students can use to buoy their well-being. Some states even require this kind of instruction in health classes. Realistically, though, most schools are not at a place where they have instituted widespread curricular change to incorporate such lessons. Many rely on sporadic programming to introduce these concepts without following up in a meaningful way.[30] Teachers, too, have expressed a desire to help, but they often feel as if they are under so much pressure to deliver content and make progress on the school's required curriculum that they cannot sufficiently attend to the emotional and psychological well-being of their students, nor do they have time to implement new lesson plans that are not directly related to the coursework.[31]

I cannot find much evidence that schools are collectively addressing the intersection of grades and mental health. To be fair, though, they are not getting a lot of guidance in this area, either. In October 2021, the US Department of Education released a report called *Supporting Child and Student Social, Emotional, Behavioral, and Mental Health Needs* that was intended to provide schools with resources to address the critical issues we have been exploring in this chapter. Although the document outlines many valuable recommendations in its 103 pages, very little of it has to do with the effect of academics on students' psychological well-being. Grades, in fact, are only mentioned twice, but there is nothing about how they contribute to the challenges outlined in the report.[32] In some ways, it is hard to extend too much blame to school districts for neither fully recognizing the extent to which grades are a piece of the mental health puzzle nor developing realistic solutions to address the issue if the nation's own Department of Education has not done its due diligence in calling attention to the connection.

What is happening to children and teens is significant, and if the relationship between grades and mental health issues is not addressed or disrupted in these earlier years, the problem can continue for students into college, where the negative effects can escalate rapidly.

The Response at Colleges and Universities

In some ways, the struggles faced by institutions in higher education are similar to those experienced by their K–12 counterparts. They seldom have sufficient funding to allocate for mental health programming, and they are often unable to hire enough counselors to meet student demand. Even if they could employ substantially more staff in their health centers, it would still not be a complete solution to this multifaceted problem.[33]

But the landscape in higher ed is also very different. Most students are legal adults, which means they are largely responsible for making their own decisions about their health. They also have the right, protected by federal regulations like FERPA and HIPAA, to complete privacy with regard to their academic and medical records. Parents cannot access any of this information unless students sign a waiver allowing them to do so. While parents can play much more active roles in making sure children and adolescents receive the care they need, their level of involvement can change dramatically once their teen leaves for college. Because college students often live away from home, it is also true that parents might not even know when their kids are struggling, which can cut off an essential avenue of support for young adults who are on their own for the first time.

This dynamic raises the stakes considerably, and colleges and universities often fall short in their response. I am usually very proud to work in higher ed. Heck, I started as a first-year college student in 1996, and I've never left the halls of academe, so I clearly find value in it. I am never more disappointed in this community, though, than I am in how it handles issues of mental health, especially because of its refusal to address how its primary mission—academics—is contributing to our ongoing crisis. We are failing our students in this area, and it is inexcusable.

Over the next few pages, I want to walk through some examples of this failure. These are difficult stories to tell, because sustained response to mental health issues in higher ed is often reactive rather than proactive. Many institutions only make efforts to put together comprehensive plans to address student psychological and emotional well-being when the circumstances have already become dire or tragedy has occurred, as was recently the case at North Carolina State University, which put together a task force in 2022 after a period of five years that saw an average of three of their students die by suicide each year.[34] Just one student death is a tragedy for any university, but more and more institutions each year are finding themselves, like NC State, facing a disaster that demands action in order to prevent further harm to students.

The university's task force issued a report in 2023 that included a number of recommendations, many of which follow patterns that begin to look very familiar the longer you explore the ways in which colleges and universities respond to tragedies like this. The report calls for more resources to be allocated for, among other things, counseling; curricular changes in required courses to add information about mental health; a series of training modules for students, faculty, and staff; and policy reform.[35] These are all, of course, necessary interventions, but they are not nearly sufficient.

There is limited discussion of NC State's academic environment, with only a cursory nod toward trauma-informed teaching practices and a few other interventions. However, the task force does briefly acknowledge the pressures of grading by suggesting modifications to some grading policies at the university level, and it deserves credit for doing so. Although the report does not address the grading practices of instructors and departments in any way, this recognition of the effect of grading policies goes further than some other institutions have gone after comparable investigations.[36]

For example, on February 3, 2022, *Inside Higher Ed* reported on seven student deaths at Worcester Polytechnic Institute during the first eight months of 2021. Three of these students died by suicide, and there were another two deaths still under investigation at the time the article was published.[37] Because of these deaths, campus leaders at WPI (as it is commonly known) rightly commissioned a task force of 35 university employees in September 2021 to study the problem and to offer recommendations for improving their support structures for students.[38]

The report, which was released in January 2022, outlines many important steps for enhancing student well-being. Similar to NC State's task force, WPI's also recommends that the institution establish better measures for identifying struggling students, more effective trainings geared toward helping students to be resilient, and developing targeted communication strategies.[39] Interestingly, the task force addresses academics as well, but there seems to be a hesitancy to do anything more than note that the educational environment is problematic.

Early in the report, the authors share information from a student survey they issued as part of their investigation. The survey, which garnered 704 student responses, revealed that up to 82% of undergraduate respondents feel there is "too much academic pressure" at WPI, and many of the most highly rated influences on mental health were connected to academic pressure.[40] This analysis led the task force to make a specific finding: "Students experience significant academic pressure for a range of reasons, including struggling to manage their workload and balancing multiple commitments. Newly enrolled students, in particular, report experiencing significant academic pressure in our introductory courses and struggle to manage workload and pace and find appropriate assistance."[41] However, the recommendations offered by the task force to address this finding do not mention grades at all. The report, in its entirety, says almost nothing about grades and the enormous anxieties traditional grading models cause for students. The silence here is both troubling and thunderous.

It is also somewhat surprising, because WPI actually has a rather innovative grading policy. The only possible grades available for undergraduates are A, B, C, NR (No Record), and I (Incomplete).[42] WPI's website does not state any particular reason for this grading system, but a generous reading of it would suggest that it was implemented, at least in part, to address some grade-related stress by minimizing the damage that low grades can inflict on a student's GPA. This institutional framework, though, is not able to tell us much about the day-to-day grading practices that students experience in the classroom, and the report itself does nothing to illuminate the ways in which these practices may be adding to the academic pressure WPI students feel so intensely.

The work of the WPI task force is representative of a trend where institutions will tie themselves into rhetorical knots by both acknowledging the pressures of academics and grades while sidestepping the responsibility to address these areas. We can see a prime example of this tendency in a February 2015 report published by the University of Pennsylvania, which had put together its own task force in 2014 following five student deaths by suicide over a period of six months.[43]

The report itself acknowledges the kinds of academic stressors felt by students on Penn's campus: "Like its peer institutions, Penn has a highly competitive academic and extracurricular culture that some students perceive to demand perfection. Such perceptions may lead to pressures to succeed both academically and socially that may be unrealistic and lead to feelings of being overwhelmed. Some experience depression or other forms of distress often evidenced by changes in behavior."[44] Just a few pages later, the task force notes that "students often have trouble coping when they receive anything other than a perfect grade."[45] They underscore the connection once again toward the end of the report as well: "poor academic performance can be seen as a risk factor for depression and other mental illness and thus faculty and academic advisors can play a key role in identifying and supporting students in distress."[46] The problem is stated more clearly here than in any of the other cases we have explored thus far. Poor academic performance (that is, low grades) is linked to the very crisis the institution is trying to remedy.

In a turn of events that will seem unsurprising to you by now, Penn's proposed solutions focus primarily on support programs and counseling. The report does not address substantive ways to reform the academic environment or the grading practices at Penn, even though it makes a pretty explicit connection between grades and struggles with mental health. I wanted to learn more about the reasons for this omission, so I emailed the chairs of the task force to ask them about their work. One of them— Rebecca Bushnell—responded. Bushnell is the School of Arts and Sciences Board of Advisors Emerita Professor of English. She explained to me that "we [the task force] saw the effects of a highly competitive academic environment and grades as only one factor in what was then seen as a difficult climate for mental health at Penn. The solution was not going to be a lowering or easing of academic standards: rather it was in seeking to change the overall climate at Penn and the ways in which we help our community respond to stress."[47]

It would be perfectly reasonable to address grades as one component of the set of solutions alluded to by Bushnell. The reality remains, though, that the task force never made any such proposals. What's more, we see here the language of "academic standards," which is often used as a red herring to deflect our attention away from the problem at hand. The assumption here is that the current culture of grading at Penn is somehow necessary for maintaining the high standards identified by the task force as being a priority for the institution, even though the report admits that this same system may be partly at fault for the mental health issues the students are facing. Putting aside for the moment what we know about grades as subjective, faulty measurements of learning, the fundamental flaws of this assumption are (a) there is no proof to support it, and (b) it provides the task force with a convenient excuse to avoid taking a close look at the grading practices and policies in use across campus.

Yet, like Penn, many institutions remain staunchly committed to this position, largely because they believe it helps them to maintain a sense of rigor. Any college or university that primarily identifies itself as being "rigorous," which is the very first word used to describe WPI in its report and is an evident priority for Ivy League member Penn as well, has a vested interest in maintaining the grading system responsible for engineering a veneer of rigor. This may be the most significant reason, in fact, for the reticence to interrogate the connection between grades and mental health concerns that we have seen in these three examples and at many other institutions as well.

But there are other potential rationales for this hesitancy. For example, questioning grades is a bridge too far for many academics because these methods of evaluation are woven into the fabric of higher education and because classroom practices are typically seen as being protected by academic freedom. Academic freedom to teach and do research on potentially controversial subjects is a vital part of higher education, but it does not and should not extend to covering teaching policies that are detrimental to students. Furthermore, acknowledging that the practices we have traditionally used in higher education might be driving some of the mental health issues our students are experiencing is deeply uncomfortable, and we may be averting our eyes in order to avoid seeing our own complicity. That is no excuse for continuing to ignore the problem, however.

It would be easy enough for every college and university in the country to pull together its faculty, staff, and students and engage them in a conversation about the complexities of mental health issues, including the role played by grades. Doing so requires very little in the way of resources and offers the opportunity to brainstorm as a community. Faculty can talk to each other about the kinds of alternative grading models I will discuss later in this book, and they can learn from staff and students about the kinds of changes that would be most beneficial. Staff, too, could hear from faculty and students about how to make workshops and other programs as effective as possible for the targeted audience. This is a problem that can only be solved together, not by individual offices in lone silos. Rather than wait for disasters to occur, institutions could hold such meetings right now as a starting point for helping their students. Sadly, most have not yet taken even this very basic step.

Where Do We Go from Here?

There is no way, nor should there be a desire, to sugarcoat what is happening to young people in this country. The magnitude of the mental health crisis can, in fact, feel overwhelming. It is possible to be so stunned by the enormity of the statistics we have explored here that we can lose sight of the fact that each one represents an individual, a young person doing the hard work of growing up and encountering significant obstacles, someone who is struggling and needs our support.

We are at a crossroads, and the decisions we make at this moment will determine what the outcome looks like for so many. This is especially true in education, because children, teens, and young adults spend so much of their time in school. As educators, we have too often become complacent, conditioned by a lack of resources and by inertia to believe that we cannot actually improve the lives of our students, but we have more levers to pull here than we realize. Closely examining our grading models and their effect on psychological well-being is but one of these elements that we have in our power to act upon. And now is the time to do so.

CHAPTER 4

Mirror, Mirror, on the Wall

How Grades Reflect and Extend Inequities

> It is one of the fallacies of justice to know that the achieve-
> ment gap is due to race and class and yet never proclaim
> racism and White rage as the source of the achievement gap.
> —Bettina Love, *We Want to Do More than Survive: Abolitionist
> Teaching and the Pursuit of Educational Freedom*, 92

By this point, we have seen that grades have a lot of strikes against them. They set up obstacles to learning, they cause undue pressure, and they contribute to the mental health crisis in our country. But we're not finished yet. Grades also serve as mirrors for the disparities that are woven into the fabric of our society, and they magnify these inequities due to their impact on the futures of the students who are affected by them.

Often used for the twin purposes of comparison and competition, grades can be drivers of injustice. Students do not need to compete with each other to learn effectively. This is one of the aspects of education that Horace Mann was worried about so long ago. In fact, any kind of competition will immediately privilege those who have played the game before and those who know the rules of the game.

The minute you begin to investigate these sorts of inequities, though, a whole host of other issues become apparent. It turns out that it's not just how grades are given that is rooted in inequity, but the ways in which grades are used in school throughout a student's educational career are inequitable as well. Although we have a lot of research on these issues, you rarely hear about them in the press or in conversations about school reform. It is time to change that.

Unequal from the Start

As with many other elements of American society, our educational systems were built on a foundation of inequity and injustice. Originally designed for white, wealthy men and then a bit later for white, slightly-less-wealthy men, schools and universities were exclusionary places meant to reinforce hierarchies rather than liberate students from those structures. Over time, of course, women and students of different races were afforded access to our educational institutions, but those victories were hard-fought and often bloody. At the University of Mississippi, for example, we just commemorated the 60th anniversary of James Meredith's integration of our campus in 1962. The days leading up to Meredith's registration for courses were marked by riots protesting his arrival and by violence that led to two deaths.[1] The roots of our history are laid bare in this and in so many other events like it. Those majority groups who wished to retain power fought, and have always fought, vehemently to protect it from marginalized groups who seek to level the playing field. Battling for full access to educational institutions is but one example of this struggle.

Access is therefore important but it does not by itself lead to equity. Just because a student can go to *a* school does not mean that school is fully integrated or well funded, nor does it mean that the educational opportunities are uniform for students everywhere. In fact, a "deeply rooted racialized structure" is a continued driver for much of the inequality we still see in schools.[2] Although integration has been a prime mover for performance gains among minoritized students, a report from 2012 "shows that school segregation for Blacks, Latinos, and poor students has returned to levels we haven't seen since the 1970s."[3] Unfortunately, higher education is in a similar boat, which means that many college students from historically marginalized groups are still being excluded, but this time they are pushed by exorbitant tuition rates into institutions that are poorly funded by states.[4] Some of these students fall victim to targeting by predatory for-profit institutions as well.[5]

How could this have happened? In the wake of *Brown v. Board of Education* in 1954 and the Civil Rights Act of 1964 that provided for enforcement of *Brown*, there was a strong push toward school integration in the 1960s, some of which depended on programs that bused students to previously segregated schools. In the 1970s and 1980s, however, a series of laws were passed that cut off federal funding for busing programs, and the states were forced to pick up the slack, which predictably led to the ending of many of these programs. At virtually the same time, the Reagan administration was putting together a now infamous report called "A Nation at Risk." Released in 1983, the report decried the state of education in the country and suggested that "our very nation was at risk because we had spent too much time focusing on issues of educational equality, racial integration, and social equality."[6] Together, the termination of busing programs and "A Nation at Risk" led to the end of the integration movement as we knew it, and schools have become increasingly resegregated in the ensuing years. The marked rise of private schools and charter schools, especially but not exclusively in the South, exacerbated these conditions even further due to what we call White Flight from urban and low-resource schools.[7]

Segregated schools are often poorer schools both because they are often located in high-poverty areas (and therefore do not have the tax structure to support growth) and also because state and local governments have always found ways to divert more resources to wealthy white communities and away from historically marginalized communities. Schools that are segregated by race and class, then, simply offer fewer educational opportunities and resources to students, and this disparity has lasting consequences for their educational journeys. This particular kind of inequity is called an "opportunity gap," and it affects academic performance as students move through the schooling system as well as the grades students receive not just in K–12, but in college as well.

Opportunity Gaps in K–12

We often hear a lot about achievement gaps in education, but we hear less about opportunity gaps. "Achievement gap" is a term used to indicate the differences in academic performance among students, and they "have been found between male and female students, among different socioeconomic groups, among racial categories, and along parental education attainment lines."[8] The problem with focusing on achievement gaps, though, is that it requires us to use a deficit lens, seeing shortfalls in the students themselves, rather than approaching the topic from the assets students bring to the learning process and the challenges they face from structural inequities they had no part in creating. Shifting to an opportunity gap model, then, allows us to turn our attention to the system itself and the barriers caused by disparities related to resource allocation and insufficient public funding that, in turn, affect some students more than others. As Kevin G. Welner and Prudence L. Carter concisely explain, "thinking in terms of 'achievement gaps' emphasizes the symptoms; thinking about unequal opportunity highlights the causes."[9]

Underresourced schools often have fewer educational materials (like textbooks and supplies), higher teacher turnover, fewer honors and AP classes, larger class sizes, and worse facilities, to name just a few of the ways they compare to schools in districts that are well funded. These deficiencies translate to fewer educational opportunities for the students who attend poorly funded schools, while their counterparts at wealthier schools get more of a chance to build skills, to practice taking the kinds of assessments that will benefit them as they move through more advanced coursework, and to navigate the kinds of academic environments that better prepare them for higher education. These are opportunity gaps. The academic performance and, therefore, the grades of the students who experience opportunity gaps often suffer, but it is because they are trapped in a system that cannot provide them with what they need.

Here is one example of how that can happen. In a 2021 feature story for the *New York Times Magazine*, Casey Parks recounts the difficulties experienced by students, teachers, and administrators in the Holmes County Consolidated School District in Mississippi. Holmes is one of the poorest rural districts in the state, and it is chronically underfunded. This is typical for Mississippi, where—as Parks reports—"nearly half the state's students attend a rural school, but its Legislature spends less than all but two others on rural instruction. This has left many of its rural districts, including Holmes, in a perpetual cycle of failure."[10] This fiscal neglect has led to significant opportunity gaps for the students in the Holmes district who are trying to carve out futures for themselves in spite of the fact that many of their classrooms do not have textbooks, and the books that are available are out of date.[11]

When students do not have access to foundational knowledge in core disciplines, it not only affects their performance in the current academic year, but it sets them up to fail in subsequent years. Students in poorly resourced schools like Holmes are always playing catch-up because they do not have the necessary materials from which to learn the key information that will set them up for success as they move into high school.

High teacher turnover works alongside limited access to textbooks to widen opportunity gaps. In the Holmes district, Parks notes, "half the instructors were uncertified, and almost all of second grade was being taught by substitutes, meaning kids showed up for third-grade multiplication lessons not knowing how to add."[12] Certainly the fact that many of the teachers in the district were untrained is enough to hamper the educational opportunities for these students, but I want to focus on the crisis in second grade. Long-term substitutes can be effective placeholders in some highly circumscribed situations, but they are not permanent solutions. In this case, the absence of consistent, committed teachers means that students are not learning the basic math skills they need to understand multiplication the next year. It is not an exaggeration to say that this has the potential to affect their performance in math for the foreseeable future. If they have trouble learning multiplication, they will not be prepared to learn about concepts like division, which relies on fluency with multiplication. Their grades in future math courses will therefore suffer, and they will encounter formidable challenges if they wish to move into more advanced math classes in high school.

This is obviously not a problem that is confined to the state of Mississippi. We find opportunity gaps anywhere racism and poverty exist, which is to say almost everywhere in America. Nor can anyone reasonably suggest that the individual children stuck in these systems are somehow responsible for the effect this has on their achievement, either. This is the bad news. Now for the worse news: these gaps not only have a serious impact on students' high school GPAs, but they have an equally insidious effect on grades for those who are able to move into higher education as well.

The Effect of Opportunity Gaps in Higher Education

When students who have experienced opportunity gaps enroll in college, they are often labeled as "unprepared" or "underprepared" or even "at risk." The reason for this unfair categorization is because these students, as a collective, are more likely to get lower grades in the introductory-level, general education courses that comprise their first academic experiences in higher education. Like the term "achievement gap," though, all of these descriptors are rooted in a deficit-centered framework. The student gets the blame here, not the system that led to the issues they are facing in their coursework.

To really understand the contours of this problem, it is helpful to look at data from specific universities. In 2021, the institutions from the Big Ten published a white paper on the grades given in their general education courses. You may know the Big Ten as an athletic conference, but those same universities have also formed an academic alliance to collaborate and share information.[13] In this report, these institutions were looking collectively at the percentage of Ds, Fs, and Ws (for "Withdrawals") across the general education courses that the universities have in common. The DFW rate, as it is known, is an important metric for equity in higher education, as it provides insight into success rates for different groups of students. We refer to these three types of grades as "unproductive grades," because they do not provide sufficient credit for advancement. Students who get Fs receive no credit whatsoever. The same is true if they withdraw from the course before the end of the term and receive a W as a result. Ds are a bit trickier. Students do get credit for a D (1.0 on the GPA scale), but it is still not considered a viable grade, since the minimum GPA for graduation at most colleges and universities is a 2.0.

Table 1 shows the results of the Big Ten study.

As you can see, the average DFW rate for each course is compared to the DFW rate for different demographic groups. Students who do not receive Pell Grants are measured against those who do receive this kind of financial aid. Pell Grants are often seen as proxies for socioeconomic status, since wealthier students are not eligible for them. Majority groups are examined alongside "URM" students, or underrepresented minority students, as are women with men and those who are not first-generation students with those who have that status. For some of the courses, like college algebra (a notoriously problematic course for students and one that is in serious need of overhaul globally), even the average DFW rate is far higher than it should be. Any course that, across multiple institutions, has an average DFW rate in the 20–30 percentile range is just simply doing a disservice to students.

Far more significant, however, is the fact that students who receive Pell Grants, minoritized students, and first-generation students have a higher DFW rate than the comparison group in nearly every course. These are the same students who are most likely to have gone to low-resource schools and to confront opportunity gaps that lead them to have fewer chances to take part in advanced coursework, or to learn from the kinds of teaching strategies they might experience in college, or to practice the kinds of note-taking skills and study strategies that might benefit them in general education courses. These gaps affect their grades, and the grades in turn serve as reflections of their educational pasts, not as projections of their potential in the present

Table 1 DFW rate (%) by subgroup for listed courses in spring 2019 at Big Ten institutions

Generic Course Name	Average	Non-Pell	Pell	Majority	URM	Female	Male	Non–1st gen	1st gen
College Algebra	32.4	30.3	31.5	27.5	33.9	28.3	36.5	28.2	34.0
Precalculus	28.1	28.0	26.6	27.8	25.3	29.5	26.8	25.9	22.5
Calculus 1	33.2	31.2	41.9	31.9	39.6	30.2	34.9	32.7	38.2
Calculus 2	23.8	23.5	28.2	21.0	30.3	18.3	26.4	23.7	23.6
Business Calculus (without proofs)	23.6	21.0	36.6	21.2	35.1	21.8	24.6	21.3	31.6
Introductory Statistics (with algebra)	13.9	12.3	19.8	12.5	21.8	13.5	14.3	12.2	20.0
Introductory Biology	15.1	12.7	25.4	13.7	25.3	14.4	16.2	12.9	22.2
Introductory Chemistry	25.1	21.1	32.9	21.5	38.1	22.3	30.3	21.2	33.5
General Chemistry 1	23.0	20.8	31.3	21.1	31.7	23.0	23.0	20.8	29.0
General Chemistry 2	16.2	14.6	25.7	15.2	26.0	16.2	16.3	14.0	25.3
General Physics (with calculus)	13.8	12.9	18.3	14.1	21.4	12.1	14.3	12.8	16.7
Physics: Electricity & Magnetism	15.0	13.3	22.1	15.5	23.1	15.2	16.7	14.0	19.0
Introductory Coding (for STEM majors)	24.7	23.3	15.4	22.1	31.7	24.0	25.0	23.0	32.5
Introductory Psychology	12.0	10.5	18.1	12.5	19.1	9.8	14.9	10.8	15.2
Introductory Sociology	10.0	8.7	14.9	11.2	14.5	8.0	12.6	8.6	16.7
Principles for Macroeconomics	15.3	14.1	24.0	13.0	23.2	14.5	15.6	14.2	20.1
Principles for Microeconomics	15.8	14.1	24.6	15.0	27.8	17.1	15.0	13.7	24.2
Introductory Accounting	14.2	13.8	17.7	11.8	22.6	13.9	14.4	12.9	18.0
Introductory English: Writing & Rhetoric	7.5	6.6	10.3	8.5	11.1	6.0	8.9	6.5	10.9
Business Communication	3.9	3.7	4.4	4.8	5.0	2.8	4.6	3.5	5.0

Source: Adapted from Kate Michaels and Jocelyn Milner, "Powered by Publics Learning Memo: The Big Ten Academic Alliance Cluster Exploring Foundational Course DFW Rates, Equity Gaps, and Progress to Degree," Association of Public and Land-grant Universities, May 2021.

Notes: The DFW rates for the subgroups are calculated as the sum of D and F grades plus withdrawal from the course after the drop deadline, divided by total census date enrollment for each cohort. Values in **boldface** are higher than the average DFW rate (*shaded*) for the course, while values without emphasis are lower than the average DFW rate (*shaded*) for the course. Course codes and titles varied across institutions and needed analyzing to group with like courses. *Abbreviations:* 1st gen = first-generation college student; Pell = Pell Grant recipient; URM = underrepresented minority.

or the future. But these students face consequences for the grades nonetheless. Essentially, general education courses, which are meant in theory to be the learning experiences that serve to open the university's doors, instead act as gatekeepers barring entry to majors, to scholarships, and to potential career paths.

Interestingly, there is a difference too between the DFW rate for women and men. Men are far more likely across courses to have a higher-than-average percentage of unproductive grades than women. While certainly problematic, this kind of gap is consistent with patterns that are supported by a wealth of research and that appear to be present as early as middle school.[14] Girls and women historically do better in school than boys and men, but they have to navigate far more obstacles along the pathways to graduation. Although some of the difference in performance between men and women may be attributed to opportunity gaps, it is likely that other factors are at play as well.[15]

The findings from the Big Ten institutions are troubling, to say the least, but they are not an exception. Lift up the hood of the car, and you will find similar DFW rates at virtually any college or university in America. The difference here is that the Big Ten is being transparent about its challenges so that it can begin to solve the problem. At the end of the report, it notes the ways in which each of the universities are responding to the data. These are the kinds of efforts we need to help mitigate the damage from opportunity gaps.

Danger: Curve Ahead

It is clear then that, because of opportunity gaps, grades can serve as mirrors for the inequities that are present in society, more generally, and in our educational systems more particularly. But one grading practice magnifies these inequities even further, and it is actually fairly common. You may have even been subjected to it in high school or college. The culprit? Grading curves.

One of the most frequently used curving models is called norm-based grading. In this framework, the teacher adds up all of the test scores and divides them by the number of students in the class in order to determine the average of all the scores. Those students who then score at or near the average get a C, those whose scores fall at increments above the average (statisticians refer to these increments as "standard deviations") get Bs and As, and those whose scores fall at increments below the average get Ds and Fs. This is true even if the average grade was, let's say, a 27%, which would practically mean that many people failed the exam, but with the curve some folks who may have scored in the 40s or 50s would get much higher grades on the exam.

You might be wondering what is going on here, and I don't blame you one bit. It is ludicrous, and there is a lot to unpack. First, let me be clear that if a test has an average score of 27%, then it means there is a problem with the test, not the students. The goal of teaching should be learning, so it follows that the tests and other assessments we design should be opportunities to reflect that learning. If the test is so hard that most students cannot pass it, then (a) they have not been taught very well, (b) the test is poorly designed, or (c) all of the above. Instructors who design exams like this often do so to create an illusion of rigor. But exams that are so difficult that many students fail them are not rigorous. They are flawed, and this is a crucial distinction to keep in mind.

More importantly, though, many who implement norm-based grading do so because they believe, or have been seduced by, claims that intelligence falls in a normal distribution in populations. This faulty, pseudoscientific framework essentially suggests that some people will always have average intelligence and ability to learn, some will have a level of intelligence classified as being above average, and some will have a level of intelligence categorized as being below average. This kind of normal distribution is commonly illustrated as a "bell curve." We call it a bell curve because, well, it looks like a bell when you see it on a graph, but also because of an infamous book by the same name published in 1994 by Richard J. Herrnstein and Charles Murray. The book, its methods, and its findings about intelligence and race are rooted in racism and deficient, partially formed beliefs about the ways in which our biology determines our destiny.[16] I do not have enough space in this book to outline all the ways *The Bell Curve* is wrong, but noted scientist and author Stephen J. Gould provides a damning critique of the book's arguments in his revised and expanded edition of *The Mismeasure of Man*, which he wrote originally to put to rest any theories that have biological determinism as their foundation.[17] Suffice to say that a grading model using a bell curve as its statistical and philosophical foundation is inequitable from the outset because it takes as its starting point the faulty notion that some students by virtue of their biology will always fall below average on the curve.[18]

The other type of grading curve commonly in use is a simpler one. In this model, which is typically applied (again) if students on the whole do rather poorly, an instructor looks at all of the scores on a test or a paper and moves the highest grade—whether it be an 88 or a 72 or a 64—up to 100 and then all of the other grades are bumped up proportionately in relation to their distance from that initial grade. So if the highest grade was, in fact, an 88, then an original grade of 86 would be moved up to a 98 after the curve was implemented. A curve like this, which I have experienced myself as a student, is often implemented under the guise of helping students. The problem, though, is that students still know that they did not do well on the assessment and that they still need to learn more. A curved, inflated grade does not change their inward feelings of failure, because they may believe they are being unjustly rewarded, nor does it help them develop the conceptual understanding they will need for subsequent courses where their grades are now likely to suffer.

Now let's return to those students who have experienced opportunity gaps. When grading curves are used, not only are these students disadvantaged by their prior educational experiences, but now they are in direct competition with students from backgrounds where they have benefited from more resources. The sort of competition fueled by curves eliminates any incentive for collaboration or study groups or any other mutually beneficial strategies to improve.[19] This only serves to widen the gaps and piles inequities on top of each other.

Inequities in Well-Resourced Schools

It is clear, then, that students who attend schools with fewer resources have the deck stacked against them, and the grades they receive during their time in the K–12 system and in college reflect this, but what about schools in middle-class and wealthy communities that have plenty of resources? Even in these institutions, as researchers have demonstrated, minoritized students experience disparities connected to their grades. These inequities are not as easy to discern, but they are felt by students all the same. In their book *Despite the Best Intentions*, Amanda E. Lewis and John B. Diamond explain that in such schools there can be a difference between the "race-neutral" policies espoused by the school and the "racialized performance" of the way those policies are enacted.[20] For example, the well-resourced school profiled by Lewis and Diamond in the book has clear procedures for tracking students into honors and AP courses, but it finds ways nonetheless to steer minoritized students into academic pathways that exclude them from these courses even when their grades qualify them and their parents advocate for this placement. The discrepancy between what this school claims to prioritize and what actually happens in practice (i.e., the racialized performance) is connected to deeply rooted and flawed assumptions on the part of school officials about the academic potential of these students.[21] Inequitable actions like this, even in schools that are not struggling, have lasting consequences on the futures of the affected students.

Additionally, Lewis and Diamond describe the advantages of white families in districts with schools that function in this way:

> White families' superior political and economic resources also combine with residential segregation to infuse white social networks with greater power, better access to and influence over school officials, and more information about the schools. In other words, as a result of structural inequalities, whites not only have more economic resources but also possess greater social, cultural, and symbolic capital with which to help their children navigate the schools.[22]

This assistance with navigating school and academics is what sets their children up for success. This is even true within different segments of the population of white families. Jessica Mc-Crory Calarco demonstrates that middle-class white families, even without necessarily intending to do so, help their children gain advantages that lower-class white families do not have. The more privileged children are taught, even as early as elementary school, to aggressively advocate for themselves in ways that others are not, and—because of this—are often rewarded with the attention of teachers.[23] Calarco notes about these children that "they got extensions on assignments. They got extra hints on tests. They got teachers to check their work for them before turning it in."[24] All of this, in turn, gave their grades a boost, but other students did not benefit from the same level of support.

Whether racial or class-based, disparities exist in all kinds of schools, even those where we might be surprised to find it. The discrimination is more subtle, less overtly detectable, but it still affects the grades of the students who are experiencing it.

Stereotype Threat

Speaking of things that are not easy to detect, psychologists have been studying one particular type of phenomenon that affects the academic performance of minoritized students no matter what kind of school they attend. It is called stereotype threat, and it is especially pernicious because students are not often consciously aware that it is happening. In a nutshell, this is the way stereotype threat works: all of us embody a variety of intersecting identities, and some of these identities are really important to us. If any of the identities that carry significance for us (gender, race, etc.) have a common stereotype attached to them, then we are at risk for stereotype threat, which occurs when someone draws attention to the stigmatized identity in a setting where we are asked to perform an intellectual task. Under these conditions, performance (on a test, for example) is affected simply because the issue is now taking up cognitive space in the brains of the students who have that identity.

The psychologist Claude Steele can be credited with shining the first light on stereotype threat. In his highly regarded book *Whistling Vivaldi: How Stereotypes Affect Us and What We Can Do*, Steele describes some of his earliest experiments related to the phenomenon. First, he studied the performance of women and men on a standardized math test. Prior to taking the test, one of the groups was told that the exam did not show any gender differences in performance, while the other group was told that women typically did not score as well as men on this particular exam. When Steele looked at the exam scores he found that in the first group—the one told there was no difference—the women did just as well as men, but in the second group men outperformed the women.[25] This result set Steele on a path that he has traveled for his entire career, and now there are hundreds of other studies on stereotype threat in addition to Steele's work all trying to find out why this happens and, more importantly, how to prevent it from happening.

We are still not entirely sure why stereotype threat affects academic performance like this. While it is possible that affected students are actively thinking some version of "I don't want to confirm a stereotype about my identity-group," it is more likely that they experience a generalized anxiety that impedes their performance and increases their cognitive load.[26] The outcome of stereotype threat is clear, though. It has a negative influence, primarily for minoritized students, on grades in individual classes and on their overall GPA.[27] Often, stereotype threat can be primed without any negative intentions, but the effect is still the same.[28] We do have some strategies that can mitigate its consequences, and we will need to use these more widely in our educational institutions if we want our classrooms to be more equitable spaces.[29]

Grades and Surveillance

I want to conclude by drawing some attention to an especially egregious use of grades, one that deepens even further the inequalities we have explored so far: the use of grades to uphold what Gavin Johnson has called a "surveillance culture" within our educational systems.[30] Surveillance is always about empowerment and disempowerment, compliance and punishment.

Who watches whom, what the watcher observes, and the consequences of the observation are fundamental aspects of surveillance. The watcher has the power and uses surveillance to ensure that those who are being watched toe the line and adhere to enforced rules of behavior.

This level of scrutiny can be found in many elements of our society, including our schools, and Johnson argues that grading can function as a "technology of surveillance."[31] Even when they seem innocuous, grades enforce compliance to a set of norms and work to punish deviance from these norms. Think about it for a moment. Elementary school students are usually given very specific marks for the way they conduct themselves, with docility rewarded with stickers and candy while unruliness is reprimanded. As students get older, grades for attendance and participation are meant to reinforce prescribed behaviors. Grade penalties for missing deadlines or falling just shy of the word count for an assignment function in the same way. None of this has anything to do with learning the material, but all of it furthers an ethos of surveillance where the teacher is charged with monitoring compliance.

I understand the reasons why teachers use grades for these purposes, embedded deeply as they are into traditional educational practices, and I have even given grades for attendance and participation myself in the past (though I no longer do so). My purpose here is not to condemn individual educators but to call our attention to the ways in which surveillance undermines trust between teachers and students. The justification for grading policies that focus on behavior and compliance is that students need such measures in order to pay attention or to attend class, but this ultimately returns us to the first chapter of this book and the importance of establishing classroom environments that cultivate intrinsic motivation. More importantly, we need students to be confident that we have their best interests at heart, and using grades for even this low-level kind of surveillance damages that.

The recent proliferation of surveillance technologies in education has made the situation even worse. We now have contrivances that will lock down internet browsers so that students cannot cheat on online tests, plagiarism-detection software that supposedly calculates how much of a student's paper is original and how much has been taken from other sources, and Big Brother–esque proctoring whizbangs that use a student's laptop camera or webcam to spy on them while they are taking a test on their computer. These proctoring programs record any movements a person makes and note those that they deem to be unusual. The supposed goal is to catch students cheating and these companies make money by convincing teachers that some kinds of movements can be flagged as possible acts of academic dishonesty. Needless to say, it is not exactly comfortable and productive for the students who are trying to take a test in this kind of environment.

Unfortunately, many educators and many institutions have outsourced their surveillance to these technologies, and you can imagine how smoothly and impartially things go when we rely so heavily on software rather than our own informed judgment. The teachers who have put their faith in these systems use the sometimes faulty and always ethically flawed data to determine grades for their students, who are viewed, at least philosophically, as guilty until proven innocent.[32] As if all of this were not bad enough, the algorithm used by at least one major proctoring company has difficulty recognizing skin with darker tones, which means that minoritized students are sometimes treated inequitably—and graded unfairly—simply because a technology cannot process their image correctly.[33]

If the purpose of surveillance is to enforce compliance, then the consequence for students of not adhering to the prescribed norm is punishment, often in the form of lower grades. Many children and young adults have internalized grade penalties for infractions that have nothing to do with learning as a part of the schooling process. For most, it has only a small effect on their education, although we cannot possibly know the impact on their psyches. For other students, though, the outcome is far different. A mother from North Dakota shared with me that her son, who is currently in high school and experiences significant challenges with attention, has been demoralized because of the way his teachers use grades to try to force him into a mold that is not a natural fit for him. He simply learns differently and benefits from deadlines that are less rigid. When he was struggling in math, she hired a tutor for him and, on his own time, he caught up with all of his homework and completed the problems successfully as well. The teacher still failed him because he had missed the initial deadline. His mother feels as if his teachers are trying to "punish the neurodiversity out of him by giving him low grades."[34] The only thing giving him low grades actually accomplishes, though, is to make him hate school. Like this student, it has always been true that children and young adults who embody differences of all kinds have been affected by the surveillance-compliance model in schools more than others, and it has reflected negatively on their grades.

While we are on the subject of punishment, educational institutions that center surveillance and strict enforcement of behavioral norms often have inequitable systems of school discipline as well, and grades factor in here too. In a recent study by the US Department of Education, which analyzed data from the 2013–14 academic year, 39.3% of all students who had received an out-of-school suspension from public school districts were Black, even though "Black students made up only 15% of the student population" overall.[35] That is an astounding statistic, but it is also one that is deeply connected to other kinds of disparities in our society. Removing students from the classroom is detrimental to their learning, however. They miss key content while they are out that affects their ability to perform well on assessments, and their grades suffer accordingly. Clearly, this vicious cycle is felt disproportionately by historically marginalized students, so what has been called a "punishment gap" contributes to the opportunity gaps with which I began this chapter.[36]

Inequities such as these have consequences, some of which go far beyond education. In 2020, Neil Bedi and Kathleen McGrory reported on a series of stories for the *Tampa Bay Times* that would go on to win them a Pulitzer Prize for Local Reporting. As part of their investigation, they revealed that Sheriff Chris Nocco of Pasco County was using data acquired with the consent of the Pasco school district's superintendent to develop a list of children who might become future criminals, according to his flawed and seriously biased logic. Although the sheriff used a number of different data points to create this list, school disciplinary records and low grades were key indicators for him. In total, 420 children were profiled on this list, which they and their parents did not know about until it was uncovered by Bedi and McGrory.[37]

This is a crystal-clear example of what social scientists call the school-to-prison pipeline and how its roots lie in fundamental inequities. In this and in many other ways, grades play a far bigger role in shaping people's lives than we often think. For some students, they are not mere letters on a report card. They are markers of stigma and concrete reminders of an unjust world.

Where Do We Go from Here?

If we were in a court room, and grades were the defendants on trial for the harms they have caused, the jury would have more than enough evidence to make a swift conviction. But it's not just the grades themselves under scrutiny here, is it? It's us too. We created grades. We continue to use them and promote their use despite overwhelming evidence that they lead to damage, and we are always finding new tools to extend the reach of grades.

Clearly, we are the problem, but that means we can also be the solution. Now that we know about the dangers, we can shift our attention to helping children and young adults reorient their beliefs about grades and to implementing strategies designed to change the system from the inside.

Let's go. We have a lot of work to do.

PART II

How We Can Help

CHAPTER 5

Building Up and Bouncing Back

What Parents Can Do at Home

> We don't have to engage in grand, heroic actions to participate in the process of change. Small acts, when multiplied by millions of people, can transform the world.
>
> —Howard Zinn, *You Can't Be Neutral on a Moving Train: A Personal History of Our Times*, 208

Are you ready for some good news? It's about time, right? Here you go: just as it is important to be honest about the realities of grades, so too can we take actions, both as individuals and communities, that can help shape a different kind of future for the children and teenagers in our lives. Despite the overwhelming evidence of the harms of grades, there are things that we can do in our homes, in classrooms, and even our educational institutions themselves to mitigate some of the damage grades can do and reframe their place in our lives.

I'm going to begin my discussion of these promising practices with some research-informed suggestions for ways to shift our parenting approaches with respect to grades and academics. As we have seen, the effects of grades are deeply felt at home, and parents are key players who can sometimes fall into the trap set by grades and put too much emphasis on their importance. If we flip that coin and look at the shinier side, though, we will see that parents also have the potential to help their kids acquire an entirely new perspective about grades, but it takes a bit of elbow grease, because it's not the easiest task in the world. Because we ourselves are unable to change whether or not schools give grades, our efforts as parents must focus on helping children and young adults to develop strategies to withstand and transform the impact of their grades.

Supporting a child who is trying to navigate an educational system that privileges grades and achievement begins, simply, with compassion and love. When children believe that their worth as human beings has nothing to do with the grades they receive, and when they know that the love of their family comes without conditions, they are better able to cope with the negative messages that grades can so often send. We must also try to remember what it was like to be a student and empathize with the difficulties inherent in our schools. Once this foundation is reinforced, then we can turn our attention to the kinds of practical skills children and young adults can use to combat the effects of grades.

Avoiding the Grade Conversation

Our first line of defense in helping our kids to recalibrate the role of grades in their lives is for us to stop talking about them so much. Honestly, the hustle and bustle of day-to-day life can make it challenging to find the time to have meaningful conversations with tweens and teens to begin with, so why waste that time discussing something that will make them anxious and has negative effects on their well-being. Talk about literally anything else related to school instead. What interesting fact did they learn in biology today? Who is their favorite teacher and why? How are their friends? How did soccer practice go? What are they reading in English class? What is the Pythagorean theorem anyway? The list is virtually endless. The key is to signal to them in the rare moments when you have quality time together that school is about far more than the letters and numbers they receive on tests.

In my family, dinnertime and rides to and from school give us our best chance to talk to Lucy about these elements of school. Right now, we're also talking a lot about friendships and what it means to be a good friend, because school is the be-all and end-all of the social world for many kids. When she encounters difficulties in academics, we find time to talk to her about that too, but we single out the particular conceptual issue or impediment to understanding rather than the grade itself.

Clearly, as we saw in chapter 2, holding ourselves back from discussing grades is a tough thing for parents to do, but doing so sends a message that we value all aspects of our children's experience with school. They spend so much of their lives there and seeing that their parents recognize how much of their personality and concept of self is developed through their interactions at school can lead to them being more receptive to other methods for lessening the burden of grades.

Managing Stress

One of the most important ways that we can help our children find their way through the world of grades is to teach them how to effectively manage their stress levels. We have already seen how grades can lead directly to stress and anxiety, and if a child's stress becomes acute, you will absolutely want to talk to a doctor or therapist about possible interventions. If, on the other hand, the stress does not rise to that level of severity but is still problematic, then there are tactics parents can share with their children so they can build healthy habits that will allow them not just to tread water but to actually thrive.

According to a resource developed by the American Psychological Association, strategies that can help children and teenagers manage their stress productively include:

- Getting enough sleep
- Exercising
- Talking to adults about the cause of the stress
- Balancing playtime and downtime
- Enjoying nature
- Writing about the stress
- Using mindfulness approaches

The APA also offers some guidance for what parents themselves can do to help their kids regulate their stress levels:

- Be positive models for managing our own stress
- Build their confidence by letting them solve some problems on their own
- Teach kids how to use media, especially social media, safely and in a healthy way
- Give them the tools to resist negative thinking[1]

If we look a bit more closely at these, we see that some of the techniques in the first category are rooted in biological mechanics (like getting enough sleep) while others offer outlets so that kids are able to process the stress. Sleep and exercise are natural methods for regulating the body and enhancing physical and psychological well-being. The problem is that most people, especially teens, do not get enough of either. In fact, sleep deprivation is a significant health issue for this population, and it has a number of detrimental effects, including exacerbating stress.[2]

Parents can assist their kids as they establish better sleeping habits by setting reasonable bedtimes, limiting screens right before bed, and prioritizing rest as an antidote to stress. I think it's fair to say that most teens and young adults need support and guidance in this area.

The suggestion to talk about stress with an adult offers parents a chance to serve as a sounding board and to provide their children with an opportunity to be heard. Once stress is vocalized it can seem smaller than when it lives in a never-ending loop inside their heads. The same is true for writing about their stress, though this might mean they do not want their parents to see what they have written, and I think we need to be okay with that, as long as they are not disclosing anything unsafe or harmful.

The second category of strategies emphasizes parental modeling. There are two here that I want to spend some time with. Perhaps the most important suggestion for parents is that we need to set good examples for handling stress. There is no doubt that this is much easier said than done, but our children look to us as models for their own approaches. Certainly, part of our approach would involve regulating our own emotional responses to stress, but we could also talk to our kids (in an age-appropriate way, of course) about what is causing our stress as a way to show them how this kind of processing can be beneficial. Crucially, demonstrating healthy methods for stress management also means being mindful of our use of substances like alcohol for stress relief.[3]

The other modeling strategy in this category involves the use of media. Part of showing children and teens how to engage with media, particularly social media, safely is to teach them directly what they need to do. Demonstrate for them how to find trustworthy websites, how to block unwanted followers, how to report harmful accounts, how to gauge the risk of posting in public, etc. None of this is intuitive, and most kids will need your help and

guidance to do this effectively. Once again, though, part of miti-
gating the potential effect of social media on stress is to demonstrate good habits ourselves. Our children learn a lot from
us about the norms for using devices, and—what's more—our
phones are often singled out as interfering with a parent's ability to interact meaningfully with his or her kids.[4] Modeling
healthy media use, then, begins by setting limits on our own use
of devices. Truth be told, this is something I work hard to do,
but it is a battle.

The other two suggestions in the parent section of the APA
guidance have more to do with fostering resiliency, or the ability to rebound after setbacks, which is an important subject in
its own right.

Building Resiliency

The Stanford psychologist Carol Dweck has spent much of her
career exploring resiliency by defining and studying what she
calls fixed mindsets and growth mindsets in children and adults.
People who have fixed mindsets believe that intelligence is static
and cannot be changed, whereas those with a growth mindset
understand that intelligence and talent are fluid and that, with
effort, they can be developed and augmented. Growth mindsets
are linked to an enhanced motivation to learn which can, in
turn, lead to greater self-efficacy.[5] In the context of grades, students with fixed mindsets are prone to seeing a bad grade as a
message that they cannot improve or that they are not cut out
for a particular subject (math teachers will surely be nodding
their heads right now as they tend to see this response with some
frequency). Students with growth mindsets, on the other hand,
tend to see a bad grade for what it is: a bump along the pathway
toward improving in a particular subject.

Parents can help their children to move toward a growth mindset in a number of different ways. The first of these strategies has to do with praising a child or young adult's effort. In her earlier work, Dweck argued that it was important to praise the effort involved in a task rather than the outcome of the assignment. Think of this as a shift from saying "Great job getting an A on that essay!" to "I can tell you worked so hard on that!" The idea behind this method is that praising outcomes and achievement leads to a child prioritizing grades and rewards while at the same time becoming more risk averse, whereas praising effort allows students of all ages to tackle more difficult challenges because they do not see their self-worth as being tied up in their academic performance.[6]

In her later work, though, Dweck has refined this recommendation a bit further to explain that it is not enough to praise effort alone or else students begin to question if they are making any headway at all. Instead, we need to praise effort "in relation to the outcome—with particular attention to learning and progress."[7] This approach places more weight on the process of learning itself rather than just pure work ethic. This means we would further shift our affirmation of their work to statements like, "You worked so hard on this, and what did you learn?" and "Your answer on that part of the test shows you are learning a lot—what do you feel like you need to keep working on?" As parents, concentrating our attention on learning seems to ultimately be the way we can move our children toward more of a growth mindset in relation to grades.

Emphasizing the importance of effort and learning can sometimes be hard given all the challenges students face in the classroom, but it is worth it. Erin, an educator and mother of two in the St. Louis area, told me that she tries to convey this message to her kids as they wrestle with grades. "We talk about effort, seeking support, and learning," she said in our interview. "We don't care about the grade as long as they put in the effort, sought support when they needed it, and can communicate what they learned. We have a conversation with [them] about whether they met both the teacher's and their own expectations about the effort that was needed to complete a task." If we make this kind of shift in our communications with our children—from grades to learning—we can provide them with some of the scaffolding they need to adopt a growth mindset with respect to their academic work.

An additional aspect of developing a growth mindset has to do with the necessity of reorienting failures and learning from our mistakes in order to flourish.[8] In the first chapter of this book, we saw how failure, setbacks, errors are all a natural part of the way we learn. We are built, biologically speaking, to make mistakes, to fix them, and to create meaning from them.[9] Trying to avoid failure, then, is really a fool's errand. It's neither possible nor desirable to do so. Instead, we need to help children and young adults to see these moments as opportunities for improvement and progress. Jessica Lahey calls this the "gift of failure," and we can give this gift to our kids so that they can begin to see these moments as steps along their educational journey rather than walls that block their paths.[10]

Dweck's work stands at the forefront of a recent movement to develop research-based models for resiliency that includes Angela Duckworth's much publicized framework of grit, Anindya Kundu's agency approach, and others. Grit, for example, is the combination of passion plus perseverance that allows people to continue pushing toward their goals even when it is difficult to do so.[11] Encouraging children to work five or ten minutes longer when they are ready to give up on a particular problem or challenge is a small step in this direction. Kundu's agency model, on the other hand, points us toward the need to tackle the socioeconomic conditions that shape a child's ability to be resilient in the first place.[12] Resiliency should not solely be the burden of any single individual or family. It is a structural issue, and nobody can single-handedly solve a systemic problem on his or her own. That is the work of communities. We need to keep this in mind even as we work with the kids in our lives to acquire the skills necessary to bounce back effectively after they encounter an obstacle.

Focusing on Strengths

Parents can support the development of a growth mindset and resiliency by focusing on and reinforcing a child's natural strengths. Michele Borba, author of the book *Thrivers*, calls these strengths "Core Assets" and says that "identifying our children's Core Assets can be one of our most important parenting tasks. It helps us honor our children for who they are, not who we want them to be. Showing our respect for who they are is the greatest way to help kids respect themselves."[13] This kind of asset-based, rather than deficit-based, mode of parenting helps to build kids up rather than tear them down because we are always focusing on what they need to improve.

Borba goes on to say that Core Assets are the "strongest positive qualities, character traits, and signature talents" that define a child. They "can be personality features such as friendliness, being a good listener, or being a smart collaborator. They can be character traits like empathy, grit, and kindness. Or they can be talents and gifts like music, acting, and original thinking. Most important: Core Assets are those that you actually recognize in your child—not strengths you hope he possesses or those you see in yourself."[14] That last point strikes me as particularly important. Our children want us to be able to see their strengths for ourselves, to pinpoint and find value in those aspects of their characters that are positive and empowering. By doing so we reinforce for them valuable pieces of their developing sense of self and enable them to feel more confident in themselves as they face challenges.

Cultivating Curiosity and Interest

Another essential strategy for family members who want to help children weather the storm of grading, so to speak, is to cultivate their curiosity.[15] Curiosity serves in some ways as a suit of armor against the damage inflicted by grades. Schools do not necessarily reward curiosity, and grades inhibit the motivation to learn, so the armor will definitely get dinged up along the way. But if parents help children to put it in place early enough, it will protect their intrinsic desire to learn and preserve their sense of fascination and wonderment.

For the first few years of their lives, children are deeply curious about the world around them. When they are babies, this curiosity takes the form of constant exploration, and as they grow and begin to talk, their sense of wonder is expressed more in the form of questions.[16] If you've ever spent any time around a 3-year-old, then you know how fond kids are of asking questions. However, researchers who study curiosity, like Susan Engel of Williams College, have shown that after the age of 5 or so, children's curiosity is dependent on the people and environments that shape their lives. If the people in their orbit do not value curiosity, then children will begin to lose the inquisitiveness that once drove their every waking moment.[17]

How do we avoid this pitfall and help kids foster their curiosity? It starts with modeling again. We need to be models of curiosity for our children, talking about what interests us, asking questions about things we find puzzling. Children look to us for guidance about the learning process just as they do with anything else. We can also indulge and support their passions. Our children become enamored with all kinds of different books, movies, music, sports, games, YouTube videos, that fall outside our own interests and realms of expertise. There was a period of time in my house where we watched the movie *Frozen* nearly every single day. And that's okay, even if it is also a bit taxing. We have since moved on to a dizzying array of interests including LOL dolls, Harry Potter, Legos, and Greek mythology. As long as the subject of their fascination is developmentally appropriate and the intensity of their focus is healthy, we should encourage these interests and even try to engage with them ourselves. See if your child will explain the different characters in the film to you or talk about why he or she loves a particular song. What you are doing for them by nurturing their passions is showing them that learning is useful for its own sake.

One example of the benefit of supporting a child's interests comes from my own family. My wife Kariann is now a brilliant artist and a faculty member in an art department in part because her mother and grandmother encouraged her to hone her skills in painting and drawing when she was a child. What began as a pastime eventually grew to a point where she wanted to pursue art as a career, and they were very supportive. This couldn't have been an easy decision for them since they lived paycheck to paycheck and wanted her to have a life more stable than theirs, but their respect for her talents and their genuine interest in her happiness made all the difference for her future. Kariann and her mother continue to have a wonderful relationship, and they both nurture my daughter Lucy's creative aspirations.

By far, though, the most important tool we can use to cultivate our children's curiosity is by asking them questions, listening to their answers, and urging them to ask us questions about any subject that strikes their fancy. If we don't know the answer, then we can look it up together, and show them how we find information and how these searches often lead to even more complex questions. All of these approaches will pay great dividends when grades begin to loom large, because they emphasize the joy of learning and the enduring power of discovery.

Advocating in Schools

I want to end this chapter by moving outside of the home for a moment, because parents will often need to take up the role of advocates for their kids as well. Communicating with teachers about a child's learning needs and strengths, campaigning against those grading portals, actively questioning reward systems, and seeking out roles in local organizations like Parent-Teacher Organizations (PTOs) and Parent-Teacher Associations (PTAs) that allow for more formalized advocacy are all important steps that we can take on behalf of our children in order to push back against a system that is obsessed with grades to the detriment of learning.

If you notice, for example, that your child's teachers are over-emphasizing the importance of grades, you can schedule a conference to talk to them about some of the research I have included in this book. A friendly email could work too, although conveying tone through email can sometimes be tricky. The key to these interactions is to focus on the issue—grades—in a productive and objective way. Teachers should be able to see parents as allies who want to help move toward a solution, not as antagonists who are questioning their professionalism.

PTOs and PTAs can be valuable avenues for advocacy as well. Philosophically speaking, these organizations should be partnerships where families and educators work together to ensure the best possible learning experience for students. This should include discussions about grading when necessary. I am not suggesting here that teachers need to yield their status as professionals in order to placate or appease parents in any way. Teachers and administrators should certainly make the decisions, but they should be transparent, parents should have the opportunity to ask questions and give feedback, and input from parents should be taken seriously even if it is not ultimately or completely implemented. Parents, too, need to trust teachers to make the best decisions for their students. Ideally, all of this work can happen within a PTO or PTA, but—unfortunately—many of these organizations have either turned solely into fundraising arms for the school district or they have become event-planning units. Both of those functions have their place, of course, but they should never overshadow the collaborative work of improving schools for which PTOs and PTAs were designed in the first place.

I approach this topic carefully, not because I don't believe in the power of these partnerships but because in recent years the political temperature in America has gotten quite heated with respect to the role parents can or should play in our educational systems. It is vital that parents and teachers are working together for the good of our children, not against each other, and assuming the best intentions of both educators and parents is a good place to start.

Why It Matters

When we put all of these efforts together, we provide a sturdy support structure for children and teenagers who must manage an educational journey during which they will face many challenges, including grades. This scaffolding, in turn, lets them know that they can rely on their parents to be their cheerleaders when they do well and can also find in their parents a source of comfort and guidance when they stumble. Importantly, it also provides kids with a foundation on which to build the skills they will need to flourish in school and beyond. As parents, we are only one piece of the complex puzzle that can lead to a solution for the grading problem, but we can lay important groundwork for success that teachers and schools can extend by making their own kinds of changes to grading practices. And as we will see, there is a lot of transformation happening in education right now.

CHAPTER 6

Reinventing Education

How Teachers Are Exploring New Approaches
to Grades and Grading in the Classroom

> There's a growing movement at this end of the second
> decade of the twenty-first century. I call it *ungrading*.
> Others call it *de-grading* or *going gradeless*. Though the
> destination tends to be generally the same, there is varia-
> tion in the routes, the reasons, the contexts, and the specific
> ways various individuals at different levels of education
> enact our changes.
> —Susan D. Blum, "Why Ungrade? Why Grade?," 2

If you were to ask any ten teachers you meet what they hate most
about teaching, you are likely to hear "Grading!" as a response
more often than not. You may also hear "Standardized testing!"
frequently as well, which is both a fair point and one that is related to the problem of grades in many ways, but we need to keep
our eye on the ball here.

Grading takes up a lot of an instructor's personal and professional time, and it forces teachers into the role of judge and eval-
uator, when many of us went into the profession in order to help
students and to serve as mentors. Grading is also hard work intellectually and psychologically. Determining the difference between an 82 and an 88 on a high school history paper is a lot
more challenging, and more subjective, than many people realize. Similarly, grading exams at any level can feel as if we are

reducing deeply complex concepts to arbitrary fact-finding missions. Because of all of this, most educators would enthusiastically agree with the idea that we need to do something about grades, but they are obligated to continue giving grades because schools, colleges, and universities require them for report cards, transcripts, student progression, scholarships, and a variety of other purposes. I know from personal experience that many teachers wonder what our educational systems would look like if grades were removed from the equation entirely.

We will tackle these systemic issues in the next chapter. For now, it is important for us to investigate some of the methods instructors are using at this very moment to mitigate the impact of grades, even while working within institutions that insist on the use of grades as the official means for evaluating students. There is a legion of educators out there doing their part to resist the tyranny of "it's always been done this way," who are enacting changes to their grading models, sometimes very openly and sometimes under the radar, in an effort to better support their students as learners and as human beings.

Remember: grades as we know them have only been around for just over a hundred years or so, and people began questioning them almost as soon as they arrived on the scene. Instructors were already finding ways to push back against prescribed grading systems even before the 1940s, which is roughly when A–F grades became the norm across the country. We have documentation, for example, of educators experimenting with contract grading (a grading model we will discuss in a moment) as far back as the 1920s.[1] That's about a century ago, if my math is right, and there have been a lot of bold efforts by teachers in those hundred years, including a flurry of grading experiments in the 1960s and '70s.[2]

So what happened? Why weren't these educators successful in creating lasting alternatives to the traditional grading practices that took hold in our institutions? Part of the reason for this lies in the ease with which traditional grading became a convenient tool to rank and evaluate students, but it is also the case that many of the teachers who were implementing alternative grading models were isolated in classrooms, schools, and colleges across the country, and those folks had no easy way to learn about nor to communicate with each other. Even Alfie Kohn's *Punished by Rewards*, which made a huge splash in our discourse about grades, did not markedly change what instructors were doing in their classrooms. It would take a technological revolution in the first two decades of the twenty-first century, along with a few key instigators, to finally bring individual reformers together as a community and create a movement.

How Social Media Fueled a New Grading Reform Movement

In 2011, Starr Sackstein was a journalism teacher in the New York City public school system.[3] Her son was attending a school that used standards-based grading, and the first report card he brought home was eye-opening for Sackstein. There were no grades listed, only marks indicating if he had exceeded a standard, met a standard, or still had some work to do to meet a standard. She was inspired by his experience to try some things out in her own classes as well. First, she stopped giving grades on individual assignments, opting instead to provide written feedback only. Gradually, she began to ask students to co-create the curriculum with her and to complete a lot of reflection assignments. By late 2014, she had taken grades out of the equation as much as possible. She still needed to report grades at the end of each marking period, but those grades were proposed by the students themselves using evidence from their work. Sackstein always reserved the right to have the final say, moving grades up or down in extreme cases, but the process was largely driven by students. Although she says that she initially tried not to draw too much attention to the changes she was making, her administration ultimately supported her work and encouraged other teachers to follow suit.

Around the same time as she was removing grades from her classroom, Sackstein was also doing some public writing about education. She was eventually approached by Mark Barnes, founder of Times 10 Press, to write a book focused on her ideas about grading. So it was that her book *Hacking Assessment* was born. First published in 2015, *Hacking Assessment* is a landmark for the new grading reform movement.[4] It is, without exaggeration, one of the most important accelerators of progress on this front, and Sackstein herself should be considered one of the prime movers. This is not simply due to her great ideas and the book's excellent reception across K–12 and higher ed. It is also because *Hacking Assessment* was one of the first books about grading whose reputation spread like wildfire on social media.

Educators make significant use of social media outlets, both personally and professionally. Through Facebook groups like "Teachers Throwing Out Grades" (which currently has more than 12,900 members) and Twitter conversations, word about *Hacking Assessment* got out quickly, and the book has now sold many copies and is in its second edition.[5] After 16 years as a public-school teacher, Sackstein is now the COO of Mastery Portfolio, where she works to build frameworks for teachers and schools so that they can reform their grading practices at scale.

Like Sackstein, Arthur Chiaravalli has also played an influential role in this new movement, largely through his work on social media.[6] Chiaravalli is currently a school administrator, serving as house director at Champlain Valley Union High School in Vermont, but prior to the pandemic he had been a teacher of English and math (a fascinating combination) for many years.

Standards-based grading also served as an inspiration for Chiaravalli, but by 2017, he had stopped grading assignments and had built self-assessment and reflection into the foundation of all his courses. That was also the year he created a Facebook page called "Teachers Going Gradeless," or TG2 as it is now commonly known. The group began with about 30 people and remained quite small for a few months, but then Chiaravalli wrote a short piece about teaching without grades that went viral and was picked up by the *New York Observer*, among other outlets.[7] That Facebook group now has more than 7,000 members who frequently share resources and classroom practices. Chiaravalli and invited guests also lead Twitter chats using the hashtag #TG2Chat that have proved to be popular for discussing challenges and opportunities related to grading reform.

A major contribution of Chiaravalli and the "Teachers Going Gradeless" community has been an openness to a wide variety of grading practices among instructors. Some educators, like Chiaravalli, have made the leap to removing most grades from their teaching, with the exception of the final grades for each marking period or semester where they are determined collaboratively, much like we saw with Starr Sackstein and her students. These are the gradeless teachers. But there are others in the group who simply want to have grades hold less importance for their students. These teachers use a variety of models, some of which you will read about below, but they do not remove grades from the picture. They are the grade-less teachers. Chiaravalli and company have embraced an umbrella approach to grading reform that invites all teachers who are exploring different models into the conversation.

Higher ed has joined the social media party as well. A lot of discussion about innovative grading practices takes place on Twitter via the #Ungrading hashtag, and David Buck—a faculty member at Howard Community College—has led lively conversations on Twitter Spaces, created a Discord site, and even facilitated a Twitter book club focused on Susan D. Blum's edited collection *Ungrading*, which itself has played an important part in moving the conversation forward. In addition, Twitter especially has proven to be a place where part-time faculty, faculty from historically marginalized groups, graduate students, and higher ed staff have been able to amplify their work with grading reform in a way that has never been possible in more traditional spaces where privileged scholars tend to dominate the discourse.

All of this activity on social media has lifted grading reform—particularly as it relates to what teachers are doing in the classroom—to a new level, joining people together from across the K–12 / higher ed divide (not an easy feat, I assure you) in a movement to upend the evaluation practices that have been harming students for too long.

Using Different Grading Models in the Classroom

I want to return now to a concept I introduced toward the beginning of the book: the idea of grading models. Every teacher in every classroom uses some kind of grading model that is comprised of the logistics for issuing a grade, the kinds of feedback provided to students to help them improve, the frequency with which students are asked to reflect on their work and their progress, and the connection between all of these elements and the teacher's philosophy about education. We have mostly been exploring the problems of more traditional grading models, but I would now like to show you some of the models that innovative teachers are using to change the game and to help students focus more on their learning. Some of these models may look more experimental than others, but all are designed to allow students to take some control of their own educational destiny, so to speak, and to give them space to develop a deeper, more meaningful understanding of the course material. Collectively, I will refer to these approaches as alternative grading models, both to distinguish them from traditional ways of grading and to underscore the fact that they fall into a separate category entirely, one that should be taken every bit as seriously as the grouping of standard models that has dominated our schools and colleges.

Portfolio Grading

Portfolio grading is perhaps the most familiar of the alternative models, and it is one that has been around in some disciplines for quite a while. In a typical portfolio model, instructors will provide a lot of feedback on student work over the course of a term or marking period, and students will have many opportunities to revise based on this feedback. At the end of the assessment interval, which could range from a few weeks to a few months, the students put together a portfolio of what they consider to be their best attempts at each assignment, and only then is a grade issued for the entire body of work rather than every individual piece. Students are often asked to provide some kind of reflective statement or a rationale for the portfolio as well. The philosophy behind portfolio grading is a simple one: students need space and feedback in order to produce their best work, and with the freedom to try out different strategies on assignments without worrying about the penalties of grades, they can take intellectual risks they might not otherwise attempt. They also have the time to develop more mature work based on the cycle of feedback they receive from their teachers. The grade they receive for their portfolio, although it is still rooted in the A–F system, reflects their growth over an entire term rather than their performance on one assignment at a time.

Portfolio grading has been commonplace in arts disciplines for quite a long time, actually, particularly in the visual arts where students work on a variety of pieces over a set amount of time and are then evaluated on their progress.[8] In these disciplines, portfolios make practical sense as a way for students to develop their creative practice.[9] More recently, however, portfolio grading has become something of a standard practice in the teaching of writing as well, especially in the first-year composition courses that are ubiquitous at colleges and universities. Electronic portfolios have now supplanted the old-fashioned folders and binders that used to be customary, but their role in helping students to demonstrate their growth as writers remains the same. With portfolios, as Kathleen Blake Yancey has said, "the self emerges, and it's often multiple, created both through diverse texts and through the reflective text that accompanies those texts."[10]

Portfolio grading models of one kind or another have now spread widely across both K–12 and higher ed, reaching even into disciplines that might not at first seem like a natural fit for this approach. For example, in a recent article Deborah Fields and her colleagues discuss the benefit of portfolios for helping high school students in computer science classes communicate effectively about course concepts and reflect on the processes they used in their work.[11] Rather than focus solely on the results of their computation assignments, they get the chance to understand their methods and practices with more depth. This is the great advantage of portfolio grading—the time, space, and feedback that allow students to extend their learning.

Standards-Based Grading and Its Cousins

One of the most promising alternative grading models is called standards-based grading. Mathematician and educational researcher Drew Lewis describes this model as "a method of grading in which course grades are primarily determined by the number of content standards a student masters."[12] So what, then, is a standard? That term is used with some frequency in education, and it can mean different things. For example, in K–12 schools, states often mandate the curricular "standards" that must be taught at each grade level. This is not exactly the kind of standard I am talking about here, though. The standards that serve as the foundation for standards-based grading are derived by individual instructors or teams of teachers and are tied directly to what students should know and be able to do in a particular course.

In their book *Grading for Growth*, David Clark and Robert Talbert define this sort of standard as "a clear and observable action that a learner can take to demonstrate their learning of some important topic or concept."[13] I would add "skill" to this list as well. In a biology class, for example, one standard might focus on explaining photosynthesis, while another might deal with knowledge about and proper usage of lab equipment in experiments. For a high school English class, recognizing symbolism in poetry would be one kind of standard and appropriate citation of sources would be another.

One key feature of most iterations of standards-based grading is that students have multiple attempts to meet the standards and, usually, multiple means by which they can demonstrate their understanding. In order to allow for multiple attempts, instructors create a process for students to keep trying if they do not meet the standard right away, often through revising their work or taking other versions of quizzes and exams. Many educators who use standards-based grading will also provide students with multiple ways to reach proficiency, such as quizzes, writing assignments, etc.

There are two kinds of grades that are given in standards-based grading models. One is used to indicate whether or not a student has met a particular standard. In K–12, a 4-3-2-1 system is often employed for this purpose, with a 3 indicating that students have achieved proficiency and a 2 meaning that they have to keep at it a little longer. A 4 usually indicates that students have exceeded the standard through exceptional work. In higher ed, on the other hand, the information provided to students tends to be a bit more streamlined. They know when they have met the standard and when they haven't yet attained it.[14] This is often conveyed through the learning management system used for the course. Final grades are then determined by how many standards students have met. School systems (for K–12) and instructors (in higher ed) decide how many completed standards are necessary to pass the class or to get an A, B, C, etc. in advance, but the grades are based entirely on that number, not on individual assignments or exams.

One of the goals of standards-based grading, as Elise B. Naramore and David K. Frangiosa explain in their book *Going Gradeless*, is "incremental improvement" over time.[15] If a student achieves proficiency right away, then the standard probably has not been pitched at the right level. The same is true if students are struggling to meet standards. Instead, students should make gains throughout the term and meet the standard at their own pace as the course unfolds. Students have a lot of freedom and choice in this system, but they are also given opportunities to learn from their mistakes rather than be penalized for them.

There are a variety of other grading models out there that share similarities with standards-based grading and are even sometimes exactly the same as standards-based grading just under a different name. I call these models, perhaps unadvisedly, the cousins. The cousins include mastery-based grading, competency-based grading, proficiency grading, and specifications grading, which involves bundles of assignments that are tied to specific standards.[16] It's not necessary to dive into the weeds of all of these, but it is worth noting that they share the core value of standards-based grading: providing students with the chance to focus on their learning in ways that draw on their individual strengths at their own pace.

Contract Grading

Another grading model that conveys benefits to students, but is more common in higher ed than in K–12, is called contract grading. Contract grading models are a bit different from the others we have explored thus far, and they warrant a bit of explanation before we go further. It is called contract grading, because early versions asked students to commit to an assessment plan they wanted to pursue by signing a statement, or the syllabus, or some other document, almost like a contract. This practice is no longer widely used, but the name remains.

In a traditional contract scheme, grades are given based on how many assignments are completed at a satisfactory level. For example, one model might look something like this: students would receive an A if they completed 15 of the assignments for the course, a B if they completed 12, a C if they completed 9, and so forth. Instructors give feedback on the assignments and make a qualitative judgment as to whether the students' work has met the assignment goals, but the grade itself is one based solely on the number of assignments completed.

Adopting a contract grading model requires instructors to clear several intellectual hurdles. First, they have to believe that students will significantly advance their understanding of the subject simply by completing an assignment at a satisfactory level. Then, once instructors have made this philosophical leap, they must commit to designing assignments and activities that will allow for this depth of learning to take place. That is not an easy thing to do; it takes time and a dedication to frequent revisions.

Contract grading is used in a wide variety of disciplines, with lots of variations on the approach I just described.[17] Sue Ann

Skipworth, my colleague at the University of Mississippi, has designed an intriguing contract grading model for her large-enrollment Introduction to American Politics course. It is useful to look at Skipworth's scheme in table 2, to see both the categories she prioritizes and the number of items within each category that students must complete to earn the respective grade.[18]

As you can see, sometimes what is required for the contract is completion and sometimes it is performance at a 70% or above. Students have a clear blueprint to help them understand what they are being asked to do and how to succeed within this framework. Skipworth's course frequently has an enrollment of more than 100 students, and she often teaches multiple sections of it, so most of the math here is calculated by the learning management system, and students can use this system to see their progress.

Table 2 Dr. Sue Ann Skipworth's grading model with four course components for POL 101 at the University of Mississippi

Course Component Expectation	Score	Attendance (absences)	Score	Quizzes (no. passed)*	Score
Exceeded	4	< 2	4	13	4
Above	3	3	3	12	3
Baseline	2	4	2	10–11	2
Below	1	5	1	8–9	1
Not met	0	≥ 6	0	0–7	0

Course Component Expectation	Score	Unit exams (no. passed)*	Score	Activities completed	Score
Exceeded	4	4	4	10	4
Above	3	3	3	9	3
Baseline	2	2	2	7–8	2
Below	1	1	1	6	1
Not met	0	0	0	≤ 5	0

*To pass a quiz or exam requires earning 70% of possible points.

Contract grading was pioneered in writing studies, and this is arguably the discipline in which these models are still the most popular. Since the 1970s, one of the leading proponents of contract grading in the writing classroom has been Peter Elbow, an emeritus professor of English at the University of Massachusetts–Amherst. Elbow's version of contract grading has evolved over the years, and he now favors a model that he has explored in a landmark essay co-authored with Jane Danielewicz. The kind of contract both Elbow and Danielewicz use in their first-year composition courses guarantees students a B as long as they complete the minimum requirements related to attendance, participation, deadlines, and revisions. Students can score above a B if their writing is deemed "to be of exceptionally high quality."[19] That final point seems to me to run counter to the general philosophy of contract grading, because it introduces more subjectivity to the model than other forms, but it does respond to any critics who might suggest that writing instructors who use models like these are abandoning efforts to enhance the quality of student writing.

More recently, Asao Inoue has developed the concept of labor-based contract grading for composition courses. The labor-based system retains the B as the guaranteed grade but centers entirely on how much work students do. They keep a journal that tallies up the minutes spent on course-related activities, and they are asked to meet minimum requirements of attendance, revision, etc. In Inoue's model, students can get an A for doing more labor—additional assignments or revisions—rather than for more polished or effective prose.[20] The driving idea behind a labor-based model, in fact, is that students become better writers by putting in the time to improve, particularly while benefiting from instructor feedback on their writing.

Ultimately, all of these different contract grading approaches illustrate how alternative grading models can be malleable in order to fit an instructor's needs and values. This is true of many of the grading schemes in this chapter and is one of the great strengths of these newer methods.

Ungrading or Collaborative Grading

Perhaps the most radical of the alternative grading models is one you have already seen in this chapter. As I mentioned earlier, grading reformers Starr Sackstein and Arthur Chiaravalli both eventually landed on a model that combined a lot of instructor feedback with multiple opportunities for students to reflect on their work and a process for students to propose their own grades at the end of a marking period or semester. This final grade is typically determined through a conference between the teacher and the student, with instructors reserving the right to change a student's proposed grade if it is too far off base or the student has not provided enough evidence to justify the proposal.

This all may seem quite new, even revolutionary, but the idea has been bouncing around for at least a few decades. In 1969, Peter Filene wrote about an approach that he called "self-grading," which seems to be similar to the strategies used by Sackstein and Chiaravalli.[21] Currently, this collection of methods is sometimes called ungrading and sometimes called collaborative grading, depending on what you are reading, although I think collaborative grading is a better label to use. As a term, "ungrading" is often deployed not only to describe this grading model, but some people also use it as a synonym for the entire concept of alternative grading strategies more generally. Still others consider "ungrading" a name for the educational philosophy that questions the role of traditional grading in our institutions.[22] Additionally, using the term "ungrading" can sometimes lead to confusing conversations where people assume that it means "not-grading" because of that pesky "un." Trust me on this.

I like the feisty spirit of a term like "ungrading," and I certainly don't think we should discard it. We will need to define it clearly, though, since words that take on too many meanings often end up signifying nothing. However, it does seem to me to be a much better fit as a descriptor for the philosophy of challenging grades, of questioning the hold of traditional grades, of seeking to upturn the business-as-usual methods that reign supreme in most schools, rather than as a word that describes the grading model we have been discussing.

The phrase "collaborative grading," on the other hand, is both more accurate regarding the practices that are central to this model, and it also conveniently avoids the conundrum of multiple definitions. Although we do not know who actually coined this term, Lindsay Masland of Appalachian State University and Jayme Dyer from Durham Technical Community College are two leading thinkers who have argued for its adoption.[23]

Instructors find their way to collaborative grading for all kinds of reasons, of course, but dissatisfaction with the effects of traditional grades seems to be a common theme. Jesse Stommel, a teaching assistant professor in the writing program at the University of Denver and an outspoken advocate of collaborative grading, has referred to this approach as "raising an eyebrow at grades as a systemic practice."[24] Stommel's point that collaborative grading is a skeptical reaction to more oppressive grading systems is an important one because it reinforces the role played by alternative grading models in rejecting the status quo.

Courtney Sobers, an associate teaching professor of chemistry at Rutgers University—Newark, shares this skepticism and has also found her way to collaborative grading. Sobers teaches general chemistry labs sections and organic chemistry lecture sections. Over time, Sobers became unhappy with what she describes as the punishing role of grades in the lab sections, particularly the penalties for being absent. Sobers moved to collaborative grading during the COVID-19 pandemic and has continued to experiment with her grading approaches since.[25]

Similarly, Nick Covington—a former high school social studies teacher from Iowa—was dissatisfied with the lack of information provided by grades about what students know and can do. He also tried a number of different grading models before finally shifting to collaborative grading. Covington left the teaching profession in 2022 and took his belief in progressive grading approaches with him to his new role at the Human Restoration Project, a nonprofit organization committed to bringing more progressive pedagogies to schools across the country through professional development workshops and other resources.[26]

While we do not yet have a lot of quantitative research demonstrating that collaborative grading leads to a greater depth of understanding and higher levels of achievement for students, we do have data showing that such models can enhance student autonomy, motivation, core beliefs, and dispositions about learning.[27] We are still in the early days of scholarship about the efficacy of alternative grading models as compared to traditional grading practices, but if students are growing in their approach to learning, as we see in some of the work coming out now, then it is not too far a leap to think that they are also beneficial for academic performance.

Boundless Possibilities

There are many other approaches as well. For example, Joe Feldman, in his book *Grading for Equity*, suggests a grading model that uses only 0 through 4 as the markers of progress. He argues that this scale is more evenhanded since there are fewer gradations and only one way to indicate failure (the zero) rather than 59 different ways to fail in the 0–100 scheme.[28] But, honestly, we have only been able to touch on a handful of strategies in this chapter, and most grading models are hybrids that use elements from a variety of different approaches. I myself have combined lots of these models in my own teaching, with a particular focus on versions of collaborative grading, and I continue to tinker with my setup each semester. Absolute fidelity to a particular model is neither necessary nor really possible, given all of the different contexts in which we teach.

In fact, at the 2022 Professional and Organizational Development Network conference in Seattle, Michael Palmer and Adriana Streifer from the University of Virginia's Center for Teaching Excellence determined that—when all of the decision-points involved in putting together a grading model for a course are taken into consideration—there are almost 16 million different ways to make our grading practices more equitable. I'm no mathematician, but that seems like a lot to me, and it certainly means that we have a huge menu of options to choose from.

The most important thing we can do, then, is to help educators find the grading models that will work best for them, their students, and their institutional contexts. For instance, standards-based grading is picking up a lot of steam in classrooms across the country, particularly in STEM disciplines where instructors want to ensure that students are learning an established body of content in order to be prepared for subsequent courses.[29] Other teachers are mixing and matching in innovative ways in order to develop grading strategies that work for their students instead of against them.

Moving Forward

I promised to be honest and open with you in this book, and I don't intend to stop now. We do not actually have good data yet regarding how widespread these practices are. I know that the skeptics who are reading this book will take this as confirmation that the teachers who are reforming their grading practices are just part of some kind of fringe movement that will fizzle out eventually, but I don't think this is the case. The proliferation of research on these different models, professional events like the annual Grading Conference that is organized by a group of mathematicians and scientists in higher ed, and the vast networks across social media that are discussing these kinds of efforts are all evidence of change and growth.[30] At the beginning of any kind of change-making process, the numbers matter less than the act of moving forward itself. The teachers who are doing this work are participating in nothing short of a revolution, a reinvention of education, and they are shifting the landscape for their students. But they cannot do it alone. To truly overturn the regime of traditional grading, we will need educational institutions themselves to change as well.

CHAPTER 7

Climbing Mountains

Changing Our Schools, Colleges, and Universities

Thirty years ago my older brother, who was ten years old at the time, was trying to get a report on birds written that he'd had three months to write, which was due the next day. We were out at our family cabin in Bolinas, and he was at the kitchen table close to tears, surrounded by binder paper and pencils and unopened books on birds, immobilized by the hugeness of the task ahead. Then my father sat down beside him, put his arm around my brother's shoulder, and said, "Bird by bird, buddy. Just take it bird by bird."

I tell this story again because it usually makes a dent in the tremendous sense of being overwhelmed that my students experience. Sometimes it actually gives them hope, and hope, as Chesterton said, is the power of being cheerful in circumstances that we know to be desperate.

—Anne Lamott, *Bird by Bird: Some Instructions on Writing and Life*, 18–19

In many ways, we've been building up to this chapter all along. Here we move beyond the home, beyond the classroom, and we take on the institutions themselves to see if it can ever be possible to break the hold of grades on our educational systems. I also confess to feeling the heat as I write this chapter, because some will be trying to find in it a Holy Grail to fix everything all at once and others will suspect that the prospect is impossible from the outset. Neither is true, but I also don't want to over- or under-sell the likelihood of change. If we have any chance of succeeding in this project, we must keep our eyes wide open and approach this work with all the realism and pragmatism it demands.

However, that does not mean that we need to be overly pessimistic, either. In fact, at the risk of sounding like Ted Lasso, the most important attribute we can bring to this work is to believe that change is possible in the first place. When you stare at a mountain from a distance and from your perspective as a lone individual, it can be difficult, nearly impossible even, to see how you might reach the top. You may think your skillset is limited or that you don't have the proper equipment or enough supplies. Once you walk closer to the mountain, though, and see the rocks for what they are, footholds begin to appear and you notice, maybe for the first time, that there is a community of people trying to climb the same mountain. Together, you learn what it will take to make an attempt at climbing to the top. The trip requires knowledge, collaboration, community, and—most of all—confidence that the summit can be reached.

Tackling a behemoth like educational transformation, especially with respect to something as entrenched as grades, can feel as insurmountable as that peak in my perhaps overly sentimental parable. It can be easy to feel cynical about the state of education today and about the possibility of true reform. But this calls to mind the necessity of hope. If this work is to succeed, then we must first move forward with the hope that it can be accomplished. In his powerful manifesto for overturning oppressive educational systems, Kevin Gannon, echoing Rebecca Solnit, reminds us that hope is an action, not just a state of utopic optimism. Going even further, Gannon suggests that creating change in education requires what he calls "radical hope," which demands from us "an assertion of faith in a better future in an increasingly uncertain and fraught present. It is a commitment to that future even if we can't clearly discern its shape."[1]

There are at least two reasons to believe that change is not only possible but achievable. First, when the COVID-19 pandemic forced colleges and universities across the country to shift their entire operations online in February and March of 2020, many of these institutions also modified their grading systems temporarily as a way to help students through such a tumultuous time. Although this was not true everywhere in higher ed, it was certainly the case at hundreds of places both big and small.[2] Some shifted entirely to a pass/fail system, where no letter grades were given at all. Others, like my own university, switched to a model where students could elect to keep the grade they received at the end of the semester or to "cover" it with a pass/fail.

I cannot overstate how radical and how quick these adaptations were. They occurred seemingly overnight, and they struck right at the core of the most traditional and inert pillar of education: grades. Sadly, most if not all of these institutions reverted in the fall of 2020 to their pre-pandemic grading schemes, but we can take from this fleeting experiment an important lesson. These hallowed halls of learning can, in fact, change. They are simply unwilling to do so, because they have a vested interest in maintaining the status quo. If they are pressured to confront the inequity of the status quo, as many are starting to do with respect to the use of standardized tests like the SAT as criteria for admission, for example, then they will begin to change.[3] This is one part of the equation that will add up to success.

Second, and just as important, we have excellent examples of educational institutions that have either recently (and permanently) modified their grading systems or never even had grades in the first place. Evergreen State College, New College of Florida,

Hampshire College, and a handful of other colleges all use narrative transcripts that are rich in feedback with nary a trace of a letter grade or a number. Additionally, an increasing number of high schools, middle schools, and elementary schools have recently altered their grading schemes, electing to provide their students with clear standards that better represent their learning along with multiple attempts at meeting these standards. To do this, most of these schools have kicked the traditional A–F system to the curb and use a much simpler scheme for communicating student achievement. If we dive in and take a closer look at some of these institutions, we can learn some important lessons about how to proceed with our efforts to make systemic change.

Gradeless Colleges

Let's begin with those colleges that do not give any grades (and have not since their inception), because they serve as important examples of how systems without grades function. As I mentioned earlier, there is a small group of colleges that qualify as being gradeless, but many of them are private institutions. Implementing any major initiative is difficult in the world of education, particularly when it comes to grades, but there can sometimes be fewer roadblocks at private colleges and universities, because they are not as dependent on state funding as public institutions are. There are exceptions to this rule, of course, but it is true more often than it is not. Because of this, I think it is helpful to take a closer look at one of the few public institutions that operates without traditional grades: The Evergreen State College, a school with an enrollment of 2,332 students in Olympia, Washington.[4]

Founded in 1967, Evergreen, as it is affectionately known to those who study and work there, is situated in a corner of Olympia renowned for its natural beauty. That it is tucked away and bordered by forests, the Puget Sound, and an organic farm only adds to the impression that Evergreen has consciously set itself apart from the rest of higher education. Indeed, the institution was viewed at its creation as a kind of pilot for innovation and change in Washington's system of higher education. There are a number of unique characteristics that distinguish the learning experience at Evergreen from that of other institutions, including the fact that there are programs rather than departments, and they do not have a traditional general education program. Students take one full-time team-taught course per term, usually earning 16 credits, although there are 8- and 12-credit options. These interdisciplinary courses are taught by an instructional team comprised of several faculty from different disciplines.

These innovations would seem radical enough to some, but they serve in many ways as complements to Evergreen's approach to grading. Quite simply, there are no grades at all—neither during the term itself nor on the final transcript. Faculty provide students with a wealth of feedback throughout the course and then, in an intense week-long period at the end of the term, they write narrative evaluations that focus on students' development and progress. These evaluations plus self-assessments written by the students themselves form the basis of individual meetings that faculty and students have during this same week, and then they are filed as part of the students' transcripts.[5]

Because of its narrative evaluation model and its other educational features, Evergreen has sometimes been referred to as a "hippie school." This label is usually intended as an insult, though it is clear from my interviews with the Evergreen community that the college values every member of its student body, so it takes some pride in the moniker even as the faculty with whom I spoke insist that the real story about the student population is much more nuanced. Certainly, Evergreen has its share of students who embody the kind of free-thinking, anti-establishment ethos that once defined those folks who were pejoratively described as hippies, but so does every institution. Evergreen's mission, however, is much broader than such a limiting lens would lead us to believe.

When I spoke to Brad Proctor, a faculty member in history at Evergreen, he said that "many students come to Evergreen because they have not thrived in a traditional educational environment."[6] Similarly, Pauline Yu—who is on the faculty in marine science at the college—told me that Evergreen tends to serve a large percentage of students who have been marginalized in the past, students who, for a variety of reasons are "more anxious about educational systems."[7] For all the reasons I have discussed so far in this book, the types of students described by Proctor and Yu benefit disproportionately from learning environments that separate the process of learning from a letter or a number, though this kind of system also has clear advantages for many students. Another benefit that both faculty members see is the reduction of competition. Evergreen students are not as focused on besting each other in the arena of ranking and sorting as we find at other institutions, because the switch that turns on this kind of competitiveness has been removed. As Yu put it, they seek to "elevate each other's work together."

Because it is so different from what they have experienced prior to attending Evergreen, some students need time to adjust to the narrative evaluation system. As Proctor explains, "A lot of students, for whom it [Evergreen] ends up being a good fit, are still really anxious and ambivalent at first," because they feel a bit out to sea without traditional markers of progress in a course. Although it takes time, most students eventually understand the value of Evergreen's approach to feedback and learning. Proctor adds that "even the students who are often [thinking] 'I didn't want grades but I'm scared because I'm not getting grades' usually end up saying this is so much better than getting grades." Some bumps along the way are expected with a gradeless system, because students have been conditioned for so long to see grades as a necessary part of their schooling, but with time they can adapt and make great strides at places like Evergreen.

But the benefits of the narrative evaluations at Evergreen are not felt by students alone. Every faculty member I spoke to at the college emphasized that the process was very time consuming, but all of them believed that the effect on student learning far outweighed the costs regarding the workload. In my interview with Stacey Davis, another faculty member in the history program, she explained that the Evergreen model "makes faculty think a lot about pedagogy and the goals of a college education and why we are doing what we're doing and not to get students to jump through hoops."[8] Davis's comments reinforce a phenomenon I discussed earlier: when teachers remove grades from the equation, it allows us to focus entirely on our learning goals and our teaching strategies.

Brad Proctor takes another tack and suggests that there are clear benefits for a faculty member's field of study too: "One real advantage is that history as a discipline is a humanistic exploration of the human past and that is really difficult to quantify in terms of what's good about it and what's not good about it, and because history still operates through primarily the written form of analysis and narrative, I think a grading model that matches analysis and narrative can be really helpful for the discipline." Proctor raises an interesting point here, and one worth considering more closely. Not only do individual students benefit when we remove the emphasis on grades to focus instead on learning. We all benefit—our disciplines, our organizations, our society— when people are encouraged to reach their full potential in environments that prioritize their development rather than their GPAs.

Whenever we talk about gradeless colleges like Evergreen, Hampshire, and New College of Florida, two common questions immediately come to the surface. One of those questions is this: without grades, do we really know that these students are learning anything? Of course, we do. No university could maintain its accreditation if it could not meaningfully demonstrate that its students were learning, and we can make a pretty strong case that colleges like Evergreen with narrative evaluations from faculty and self-assessments from students actually have far more specific information about learning than institutions that rely primarily on grades as data. These narratives provide insight into what students actually know and can do, which is not something easily conveyed by a letter grade or a number, even if it is paired with a paper or test or project as evidence of students' work.

The skeptics out there will also be thinking about content mastery and conceptual understanding as they ponder this question about student learning. When I speak to groups of educators on the subject of grades, someone—usually a specialist in the health sciences—will say to me, "This is all fine and good, Eyler, but if my students don't know [fill in the blank with an important idea/concept/technique] by the time they graduate, then people will DIE!" What I see in this kind of extreme defensiveness is a worry about the value of expertise and about the importance of science, both of which are absolutely essential for building a better world. So I empathize with those who respond to me in this way, even if it is not a particularly fun exchange. But their reaction stems from a fundamental misunderstanding. Just because there are no grades does not mean that there are no academic standards. Scientists at Evergreen, like Pauline Yu and Krishna Chowdary (who teaches physics), carefully craft mechanisms for determining whether or not students have reached or exceeded proficiency with respect to the content for the course.[9] This kind of assessment can happen in exams, projects, in-class work, or problem sets completed by students outside of class. An approach to student learning, especially in STEM courses, that centers a more in-depth demonstration of understanding takes time and patience, but the faculty at Evergreen prove that it is possible.

The second question about gradeless colleges follows quickly on the heels of the first: how do these students fare after graduation? Evergreen students get into graduate schools, medical schools, and law schools just like students at every other institution, and they are employed in all the same industries.[10] It takes more time to read an Evergreen transcript, but this does not seem to be a deterrent, and—according to the college's website— the registration and records office can provide summary versions as needed.[11] David McAvity, Evergreen's interim provost, told me that "when you are doing something different from everyone else, then you are going to have some friction as you rub up against the norms," so they will sometimes have cases where a fellowship application or an internship or an offer of admission at another institution hinges on having an actual GPA calculated.[12] As a last resort, Evergreen has a mechanism for making this calculation and will do so for the benefit of the student in these situations, but the need for this seldom arises. By and large, Evergreen has had great success making narrative transcripts work for its students.

Evergreen's story is an instructive one. It not only gives us a blueprint for what a gradeless institution looks like and how it functions, but it also shows us what is possible when an entire college focuses on learning rather than grades. While Evergreen is not alone in its pursuit of this mission, it does need reinforcements.

Building Gradeless Programs

It is one thing to look closely at institutions that have always been gradeless, but the stakes shift significantly when we begin to talk about changing from a system with traditional grades to one without grades. I have not seen entire colleges and universities make this leap (yet!), but there are individual programs moving in this direction. Consider, for example, the University of California, San Diego, which is made up of a series of undergraduate colleges. These colleges at UC San Diego contain both an academic program, comprised primarily of the general education requirements, and residential life resources. Each college has a theme that drives the academic work, and students are encouraged to enroll in the college that fits them best.

In the fall of 2020, the first group of students matriculated into Seventh College, which is—unsurprisingly—the seventh and most recent undergraduate college to open at UC San Diego.[13] The academic theme at Seventh College is "A Changing World," and this central idea inspired Jill Gladstein when she was hired to design the writing program for its students. While the rest of the academic program at Seventh College is graded more traditionally, Gladstein investigated changes that were happening across the higher ed landscape, including those related to grades, and decided that the Synthesis Program, which is what they call the writing curriculum in Seventh College, should be at the leading edge of these changes. I recently spoke to Gladstein about the grading model she developed from scratch for the program and about her reasons for doing so.[14]

The Synthesis Program is made up of three required courses: SYN 1, SYN 2, and SYN 100. SYN 100 is a project-based course that can only be taken after students complete the first two courses. SYN 1 and SYN 2 are composition courses where students build their skills in argument, evidence, close reading, and revision, among others. Gladstein's first step was to pilot in SYN 1 a contract grading model where the grades students receive are based on how many assignments they complete and how much work they put into revising their writing using the feedback from the instructor. The grading model of SYN 2 asks students to do a lot of self-assessment over the course of the term and then make an evidence-based case for the final grade they should receive. The grade that goes in the books is then determined in conjunction with the instructor. SYN 100 then continues with a model similar to that used in SYN 2.

Although it would appear that the courses are using slightly different approaches to grading, Gladstein has placed all of these practices under the umbrella of collaborative grading, which adds a bit of a spin to the term that we explored in the previous chapter. The contract grading that students see in SYN 1 is the first step in a collaborative scheme that introduces students to progressive models, and then they move toward having additional agency in SYN 2 and SYN 100, where they are taking a more active role in determining their final grade. Gladstein's move to join the two types of grading together is smart both philosophically and pedagogically. Doing so provides an important scaffold that allows students to begin their work as college writers even as they are also taking more ownership of their education.

Gladstein is quick to point out that, although she is the director, the courses themselves are primarily taught by graduate students from across the disciplines. She credits them with much of the success of the program, but she also notes that together they all had to "unlearn" their own assumptions about grades, evaluation, and learning before the Synthesis Program could really get up and running. Fortunately, Gladstein had administrative backing for the changes she made as well. UCSD prides itself on educational innovation, she told me, so her ideas were not a tough sell for Seventh College's provost, though she does expect that the assessment process for the program will prompt more feedback as it unfolds.

The Synthesis Program at UCSD is a rare case of system-level transformation with respect to grades in our colleges and universities, although there are bright spots on the horizon. Elsewhere in the University of California system, for instance, there are campuses that are contemplating the removal of traditional grades for first-year students and even some individual departments that are moving holistically toward progressive grading models.[15] Overall, though, these stories of change are few and far between. As I mentioned at the beginning of this chapter, this reluctance to change has much more to do with will than it does with capability. It is more common, particularly over the last decade, to see these kinds of changes attempted in the K–12 world than in higher education. This is certainly true of individual schools, but I want to focus on the large-scale initiatives at the state level and in school districts. Not every attempt has been successful, but we can learn just as much from those that went awry as we can from those that prospered.

Change at the State Level

First, let's take a peek at some states that have tried to challenge the status quo regarding grades. As it happens, the northeastern corner of our country has spent much of the last decade riding the rollercoaster of legislative action and district implementation with respect to grading policies. I went to graduate school in New England, and while I remember it having lovely foliage and cold winters, I don't recall it ever being a battleground for educational reform. Yet Maine and Vermont have been out in front as they attempted to move all of their schools toward proficiency-based grading, which we learned in the last chapter is a cousin of (and sometimes a synonym for) standards-based grading and competency-based grading.

In 2012, Maine passed a law mandating that all school districts in the state needed to move from traditional transcripts with A–F grades to a proficiency-based diploma by the time the class of 2021 graduated. The focus of the law was equity, a more accurate demonstration of student knowledge, and preparation for Maine students to be more competitive in their future academic pursuits and their careers.[16] Vermont passed a very similar law in 2013, though for slightly different reasons. The state legislature wanted to offer the opportunity for students to get credit for learning via avenues besides formal schooling, such as work-based learning.[17] They called these opportunities flexible pathways, and proficiency-based diplomas were viewed as a primary means for making these pathways a reality. To be sure, equity and grade reform were major considerations, but they were not the primary emphases. Because proficiency-based diplomas necessarily involve grades, though, they quickly stole the spotlight (and, arguably, the resources) from flexible pathways.

You're probably wondering what the result of this experiment has been. That's fair, and I won't make you wait any longer. Vermont, that small but feisty state, is still going strong. Although a bill was introduced in the legislature in 2021 to make proficiency-based diplomas optional, there is no evidence that it has ever made it out of committee.[18] Maine, on the other hand, has been something of a disaster. In 2018, the state passed a new law undoing the work of the first, making it now optional for school districts as to whether or not they wanted to continue pursuing proficiency-based education. Although there were objections that such a move would undo the substantial progress that schools had already made toward equity, the law has effectively led to many districts abandoning the program.[19]

Both states delegated the responsibility of implementing the reforms to the local school districts. Regarding Maine, scholars from the University of Southern Maine have explained that as recently as 2018, it was "evident that the emphasis on local decision-making in how to interpret and implement the law was resulting in substantial variation from district to district," and the result of this was a rather chaotic and widely disparate implementation.[20] On the surface, the situation in Vermont looks similar. Its Agency of Education has a webpage devoted to explaining how each school district has implemented proficiency-based programs and the details regarding what the reforms look like in each district.[21] They all look different, and some even translate the proficiencies into traditional grades for the transcript, but they were given the flexibility to do so by the state.

The key differences seem to be that Vermont's Agency of Education offered quite a few centralized resources, including clear options for what the transcript could look like as well as common definitions of terms and ideas related to proficiency-based education.[22] Maine's implementation, on the other hand, "was compounded by challenges and delays in the development of uniform regulatory guidance from the Maine Department of Education; to date, no final rules have been released."[23] Clearly, the bureaucratic disorganization in Maine only served to reinforce the perception among some school leaders and politicians that the state was never serious about the program to begin with. Conversely, the state-level support in Vermont provided a bit of a beacon as school districts tried to navigate their way through what was obviously a sizable change.

Furthermore, Vermont did more to equip its superintendents, principals, and teachers with tools for working with the parents in their districts.[24] Parents and family members are the key demographic for making this level of change possible. They need to understand why schools would want to shift away from traditional grades, they need frequent communication, and they need to know how any alterations of the grading model will affect a child's chances to get into their college of choice. Any overhaul to grades will fail without the support of parents and other family members, and this is one of the biggest reasons that the implementation failed in Maine. By many accounts, the communication with parents in that state was poor, and they organized their efforts to protest the turn toward proficiency-based learning.[25]

Maine is certainly something of a cautionary tale, but its failures should not be taken as evidence that all such efforts are doomed to fall flat, because its fellow New England state offers us a different narrative. Instead, we need to reckon with the mistakes made by leaders in Maine and try to understand them from the inside out so that we can avoid them in future initiatives.

Changing Schools and School Districts

When we move away from the state level and look instead at individual school districts that have attempted to change the way they grade, we see similar opportunities and challenges. I want to focus now on one such district: Elmwood Park Community Unit School District #401, located in a suburb of Chicago with a population of about 25,000 people.[26] Although it has not been easy, this district has shifted bit by bit to standards-based grading, and exploring the moves the leaders and teachers made as they went about this work adds considerably to what we learned from the efforts in New England.

Elmwood Park CUSD is captained by superintendent Leah Gauthier, who began her career as an elementary school teacher before taking on other positions like math specialist, learning coordinator, instructional coordinator, director for curriculum and instruction, and assistant superintendent for curriculum and instruction. She was named superintendent in 2020. In other words, Gauthier has really done it all, and she has long been a champion of grading reform. When we spoke about her school district's move to standards-based grading, she told me that during her time as a teacher she noticed that the love of learning wanes as kids grow older, and she watched her fellow teachers struggle with this.[27] As she moved into administration, she wanted to empower teachers to enhance intrinsic motivation in their classes and to provide them with the support they needed in order to make this work sustainable.

She is now in her fifth year in Elmwood Park CUSD, but when she arrived as an assistant superintendent, the idea to shift to standards-based grading was a new one and implementing it was immediately added to her areas of responsibility. Her prior experience in a system that used this grading model had prepared her for the task at hand, but she still felt as if the change would be a bit tricky since Elmwood Park's schools did not yet have common assessments, common grading practices, or even a common curriculum shared by teachers. As you will recall from the previous chapter, standards-based grading depends on breaking down instructional content into benchmarks that demonstrate a student's progress in each area and then evaluating student work often using a scale that looks something like this: 4 (exceeds the standard), 3 (meets the standard), 2 (does not yet meet the standard), and 1. Clearly, then, Gauthier had a big job ahead of her.

She began by bringing together educators from across Elmwood Park's four schools to design collaboratively a "portrait of a graduate." They discussed what they wanted their students to know and to be prepared for by the time they left the district. These characteristics then became a kind of north star for them as they worked together to begin the process of aligning their curriculum for kindergarten through twelfth grade. By bringing the district's teachers into the process at such an early stage,

Gauthier achieved two important objectives. First, she was able to dispel the notion that this was solely a top-down initiative, and second, the teachers were given agency in the process and were more invested in it as a result.

In the 2017–18 academic year, the district focused on researching and refining every element of the K–12 curriculum and aligning this new curriculum with the specifications laid out in the Illinois Core (the state's version of the Common Core). The new curriculum, fully aligned, was then piloted in summer school in 2018 and launched throughout the K–12 system at the beginning of the 2018–19 academic year. Notice that we haven't talked about grades yet. That is because Gauthier wanted to focus first on getting the collaboratively designed curriculum to a point where the teachers agreed with its goals and supported its implementation.

Only after the full launch of the curriculum did Gauthier begin to open up the conversation about grades. The district dipped its toe into the waters of discussing common grading practices by prioritizing professional development for the schools' teachers and administrators, again acknowledging that a successful process would depend on equipping teachers with as many tools as possible and allowing them to lead from within. Gauthier funded book studies for teachers to talk about the research behind grading reforms and the practices that drive these efforts, and 60 educators took part in specialized training workshops on standards-based grading. As a result, 2018–19 was dedicated to building priority standards and proficiency scales for every level from kindergarten to twelfth grade and to developing a report card prototype as well.

In 2019–20, with the priority standards and proficiencies thoroughly established, standards-based grading was at long last piloted in every classroom, and standards-based reporting, via the new report card model, was piloted in K–5. The distinction here is an important one. While standards-based grading was used for assignments, activities, exams, etc. throughout the district, only K–5 classrooms were using the 4-3-2-1 scale on the report cards themselves. The reason for this is one of logistics. Gauthier and her colleagues wanted to have an opportunity to refine the report card before introducing it to middle school and high school, where the stakes are significantly higher and the power of traditional grades more intense. She did set the stage for success in these other levels, though, by bringing those teachers into the conversation early on, by developing the standards and the proficiencies in advance, and by training the teachers in standards-based grading from the outset of the initiative. After a brief hiccup due to the pandemic, the report cards are now finalized for K–6 and will be implemented in a new grade level each year.

Another component that fell into place in 2019–20 was the creation of a districtwide committee made up of teachers and parents to act as an advisory board of sorts for the standards-based initiative. This, on top of the numerous information sessions about the process for parents, went a long way to smoothing out any potential roadblocks before they could even occur. Gauthier and her staff understood that communication with parents and an investment in resources for parents were vital for the initiative to be successful, and it is no small part of why they have come so far so quickly.

Leah Gauthier, her staff, and her teachers began the work of grading reform at square one and had to weather a pandemic and jump over logistical hurdles along the way, but it has worked. Elmwood Park offers educators and parents everywhere an important case study for how to make systemic change in our schools.

Each year, more and more districts are making similar changes to their grading models, often electing, like Elmwood Park, to transition to standards-based grading. Santa Fe Public

Schools, a district in New Mexico, is in the process of converting schools to this system and will see the first full-scale implementation in the 2022–23 academic year. Their decision to do this was made, in part, because of the learning experiences of their students and teachers during the pandemic.[28] Other districts, like Lindbergh Schools in St. Louis, Missouri, are in an earlier stage of the process, but they are moving full steam ahead.[29] Whether or not their efforts flourish will depend on the right combination of strategy and commitment.

A Blueprint for Change

Clear patterns emerge both from the initiatives that succeeded and those that faltered along the way. These lessons can provide a blueprint for those who seek to make change in their own school districts or institutions, and they are consistent with what scholars have observed about similar reform efforts in the past. Thomas Guskey has spent his career studying attempts at grade reform, and in a recent article he outlined some of the most important elements for helping sustainable change to take root:

- Begin with transparency
- Take things in order
- Describe "why" before "what"
- Anticipate and address opposition[30]

What ties these pieces of the puzzle together, according to Guskey, is strong leadership. Certainly, we've seen in the examples I have shared the necessity of strong, clear-sighted leadership, especially regarding the first two of Guskey's key elements. Transparency starts at the very top. Maine failed in its statewide efforts to be transparent, from its mixed messages to school leaders to its inattention to parents. On the other hand, Leah Gauthier at Elmwood Park CUSD emphasized transparency and deliberative decision-making at every turn.

Leaders do not dwell only on the highest rungs of the institutional ladders, though. There are leaders at every level in a school, college, and university, and these folks are crucial for any reform efforts. Coordinated attempts at changing institutions will often require a cohort of teachers who are willing to be the first to try something new, as well as a coalition of others (sometimes the same crew, sometimes not) who can carry the practices onward even when doing so means they will be challenged by students, colleagues, community members, and others. These instructors are leaders in their own right and deserve credit for it. Their efforts will only go so far, though, if they do not also have people in positions of power sponsoring their work, advocating for change, and drawing the notice of superintendents, provosts, and presidents. This category of leader is often found among principals, department chairs, deans or assistant deans, and associate or vice provosts. All are crucial elements of the equation that results in change.

Guskey's framing of putting the "why" before the "what" is an important driver of change as well. Both Maine and Vermont put the "what" before the "why" in many ways. Legislating a move to proficiency-based diplomas is the very definition of a top-down approach and essentially tells people what to do but not why to do it. When you read the laws that both passed, you do see some of this rationale, but it is clear that the "why" here did not often make it down the chain to the teachers who were tasked with implementation. Vermont did a better job of communicating this after the fact, but its early mistake could have cost them every bit as much as it cost the residents of Maine. Educators are often drawn to the profession because they care about students and about learning, so they are going to work hardest to help those programs succeed that they believe in first and foremost. The "why," in other words, is everything to educators, but it is too often overshadowed by the bureaucratic "what" of the initiatives they are asked to put into place.

The most interesting part of Guskey's list of key factors is the notion that we have to head the "opposition" off at the pass. Who falls into this category, though? Although Guskey does not include this group in his framework, sometimes the very people we are trying to help—the students themselves—oppose efforts to implement new models. When students resist change, it is usually because they have spent so much time in a system focused on traditional grading that they don't know what the alternatives would even look like or why change would be necessary. More often than not, though, students are our biggest allies for change. Once they understand the reasons for grading reform, they will often stand alongside us, making the case to administrators and other teachers for the necessity of new models.

Guskey does suggest that there may be pockets of educators who resist changes to traditional practices that are deeply rooted in their belief systems about education, antiquated though those systems may be.[31] I don't want to cast too much blame in this direction, though. Teachers and faculty members are torn in lots of different directions on a daily basis and are often given little support. Part of the survival mechanism is to deflect instinctively anything new coming down the pike. Also, this sort of conflict is rarer than we might imagine. Most people who stand in front of the classroom are genuinely interested in helping students learn and succeed.

Finally, we come back to the parents who are so important to reform efforts. They are also included in Guskey's opposition group, but I don't see them in the same light.[32] Parents simply care about their children. They don't always know the inside baseball of the world of education, and they can sometimes express their concerns unproductively, but it comes from a place of care. One issue frequently tied to the parental concerns I heard as I interviewed people for this book was the fear that students would not be admitted to competitive colleges if they graduated from a high school that did not have traditional grades or standard transcripts. This worry was shared by administrators and teachers as well.

I wanted to find out whether or not there was any real cause for this concern. My instinct, from serving as an administrator in higher ed for more than a decade, was that this probably was not as big a deal as people were assuming it was. Why could I be so confident? Most colleges and universities, quite simply, are not looking for extra reasons to turn students away. Many institutions need higher enrollment numbers to boost their revenue and to stay afloat. But also: if nontraditional transcripts were really such an issue, then no homeschooled student would ever be admitted to college, and—according to the most recent data available from the Department of Education—there were nearly 1.7 million homeschoolers in the United States in 2016.[33] That number may have even been as high as 2.6 million before the pandemic hit in 2020, too, so we are talking about a lot of students who are applying to college from this pool and are doing just fine.[34]

Furthermore, I spoke with James Corner, who is an assistant director of admissions here at the University of Mississippi, about how he and his colleagues handle nontraditional transcripts when making decisions about admissions.[35] According to Corner, they translate the transcript by using "the ledger/rubric provided by the institution. If a rubric is not included with the transcript, we contact the school's counselor for guidance." I specifically asked him about standards-based or proficiency-based transcripts, because these are the models most widely adopted by high schools interested in grading reform. He reported that there were "not many challenges in translating" these kinds of transcripts and that the students who were applying from schools with nontraditional transcripts were just as competitive for admission as those from schools with more traditional grades. Although it would be a stretch to say that they were being flooded with standards-based transcripts, it was clear from my conversation with Corner that these kinds of applications were not unusual.

The picture is not entirely rosy, however. A director of admissions at an Ivy League institution (who asked not to be named) said that the biggest potential obstacle for applications that include a nontraditional transcript is the amount of time it takes to read them.[36] Admissions officers at this university, and at most other universities, must work through a gobsmackingly large number of applications each day, and anything that throws off the pace of reading can be a hindrance.[37] This director also explained that the applicant's supporting materials—such as letters of recommendation, essays, etc.—would carry significant weight to add more context to the transcript. In the same interview, however, I was told that the great majority of students who are applying to the Ivies have such high GPAs that the rest of the application materials matter more in the end anyway. A student with a nontraditional transcript, then, is basically in the same boat as everyone else, and parents, teachers, and administrators should take enough comfort in this to place less pressure on the type of grading model used by their schools.

I understand this fundamental concern and many other parental worries as well. I think about them when I consider my own daughter's future. But when I look at all of the evidence before me, and I see all of the hard work that K–12 teachers, college faculty, and administrators at every level are doing to change our educational systems for the better, I know that the hard work of grade reform is as possible as it is necessary.

When I worked at Rice University, I had a colleague named John Hutchinson. John's email signature always included the quote, "Nothing happens until you do something." I've taken that sentiment to heart: change requires action. In the case of grades, we will need collective action and the power of community to transform our educational systems.[38]

It is past time for us to begin this work, but it is not too late. We must build on the progress that others have already made and prioritize our children and young adults over the mirage of rigor and the inertia of the status quo. If we are not meaningfully working to reshape the role of grades in our schools, colleges, and universities, then we are complicit in a system that is doing students harm. Their happiness, well-being, and opportunities for lifelong success matter far more than our unwavering allegiance to decrepit educational practices that have long since revealed their dangers and their hollow promises.

Epilogue

A Future without Letters?

Come along, Madame Hester, and show your scarlet letter
in the market-place!
—Nathaniel Hawthorne, *The Scarlet Letter*, 40

We haven't talked much about Nathaniel Hawthorne since the beginning of this book, but I would like to bring our old pal and his work back into our conversation once again before you and I say farewell. Children, teenagers, and young adults carry their grades with them, like so many Hester Prynnes, as they grow older and begin to make their way in the world. Long after they graduate from high school or college, they wear their letters still, internalizing the stories they believe their grades have told about them. Often these messages distort their ability to see within themselves their own potential and possibility. Though the grades themselves are visible to no one, they fester and scar nonetheless.

As a teacher, I have worked with so many students who feel intensely the burden of their scarlet letters. By the time I have the privilege of working with them in college, their grades have already transformed into obstacles they believe they cannot overcome. They see their grades as defining them, their intellect, and their ability to have a career where they can contribute positively to society. They feel as if they have been marked as an "A student," a "C student," as "not a math person." The letters so quickly become entwined with their identities, and they are defeated before they have even begun. Maybe this story even feels familiar to you yourself.

As a parent, I have tried to help my daughter fight against a culture that places these letters above education itself. I want her to experience the beauty and power of learning something new simply because she is interested in a subject, not because she needs a particular score on an exam. My greatest hope for her, in fact, is that she discovers a field of study she is as passionate about as my wife is about art and that I am about education, and I worry that the intensity of grade-obsessed schools will stifle the curiosity and drive that are necessary for this kind of revelation before they are even allowed to develop.

It doesn't have to be this way, though. Remember that the A–F grading system was only adopted widely in the 1940s, so nothing about it has ever been inevitable. What's more, advocates have been fighting back against grades in one way or another since their inception, and they have made important gains that we can build on. There is hope yet, and now is the time to act on it. Even if it seems too idealistic to believe that we can get rid of grades once and for all, we *can* make changes in our local context. We have seen, within these pages, examples of the pioneering schools, brave educators, and loving parents who are doing just that day in and day out.

But why not aspire to something better? Why not dream of revolution? Why not imagine a world where children have the freedom to learn without judgment, to explore without fear, to seek without consequence?

We can dream this dream together.

Notes

Preface

1. See Eyler, *How Humans Learn*, 171–217.

Introduction

1. For more on the distinction between these two terms, see Suskie, *Assessing*, 12.
2. The most influential study that, among other findings, connects grades to feelings of self-worth is Crocker, Luhtanen, Cooper, and Bouvrette, "Contingencies of Self-Worth," 894–908, especially 906. Crocker and another group of colleagues looked specifically at the interplay between negative self-worth and grades for engineering and psychology majors. See Crocker, Karpinski, Quinn, and Chase, "What Grades Determine," 507–16.
3. Schneider and Hutt, "Making the Grade," 201. I'm excited to report that the Latin translations are my own.
4. Stray, "Shift from Oral to Written," 36–37.
5. Brookhart et al., "Century of Grading," 805.
6. Davidson, *New Education*, 204–5.
7. Schneider and Hutt, "Making the Grade," 206.
8. Mann, *Ninth Report*, 142–43.
9. Particularly in his *Seventh Report* (165–70) and in his lecture "The Means and Objects of Common School Education" (47–49).
10. Mann, *Tenth Report*, 196–97.
11. An article from 1931 makes the direct link from Mann to the development of report cards: Holland, "Pupil Reports," 363. Similarly, Robert

149

Talbert also noted Mann's important role in the development of report cards and his vital position in the history of grading reform in a blog post called "Who Was Horace Mann?"

12. See Morris, *Report Cards*, 12–23, for a history of the development of report cards in the 1800s.

13. American Montessori Society, "Montessori FAQs."

14. National Center for Montessori in the Public Sector, "About Montessori."

Chapter 1. The Race Nobody Can Win

1. Bain, *What the Best College Teachers Do*, 34.

2. Kohn, *Punished by Rewards*, 3–18.

3. Deci and Flaste, *Why We Do What We Do*, 9.

4. Deci and Flaste, *Why We Do What We Do*, 9.

5. Cerasoli, Nicklin, and Ford, "Intrinsic Motivation and Extrinsic Incentives Jointly Predict Performance," 996.

6. Butler and Nisan, "Effects of No Feedback, Task-Related Comments, and Grades," 211.

7. Butler and Nisan, "Effects of No Feedback, Task-Related Comments, and Grades," 215.

8. Butler and Nisan, "Effects of No Feedback, Task-Related Comments, and Grades," 215.

9. Koenka et al., "Meta-Analysis on the Impact of Grades and Comments on Academic Motivation and Achievement," 935.

10. Koenka et al., "Meta-Analysis on the Impact of Grades and Comments on Academic Motivation and Achievement," 935.

11. Pulfrey, Buchs, and Butera, "Why Grades Engender Performance-Avoidance Goals," 696.

12. Pulfrey, Buchs, and Butera, "Why Grades Engender Performance-Avoidance Goals," 683.

13. Ryan and Deci, "Intrinsic and Extrinsic Motivation from a Self-Determination Theory Perspective," 2–3.

14. The podcast episode was released on October 14, 2020. *Tea for Teaching* is hosted by John Kane and Rebecca Mushtare.

15. Anderman and Koenka, "Relation between Academic Motivation and Cheating," 97.

16. Whisenhunt, Cathey, Hudson, and Needy, "Maximizing Learning while Minimizing Cheating," 142.

17. Lang, *Cheating Lessons*, 13–16.

18. I have used a pseudonym here to protect his identity, and I use similar pseudonyms throughout the book for all children under the age of 18. Interviews with minors were only conducted after I acquired consent from both the interviewee and one of her, his, or their parents. This interview was conducted on October 27, 2019.

19. Eyler, *How Humans Learn*, 177–78.

20. Ross et al., "Instructor Perspectives on Failure and Its Role in Learning in Higher Education," 95.

21. Campbell and Cabrera, "Making the Mark," 504.

22. Brookhart et al., "Century of Grading," 834–35.

23. Singh, "Grading Gets an F."

24. Quinn, "At Michigan, Getting an A because Your Instructor's on Strike."

25. See, for example, Starch and Elliott, "Reliability," 442–57. Their articles on grades in math and in history classes appeared the next year.

26. Kohn, "Dangerous Myth of Grade Inflation."

27. V. Johnson, *Grade Inflation*.

28. Bar, Kadiyali, and Zussman, "Grade Information and Grade Inflation," 106.

29. Clune, "AI Means Professors Need to Raise Their Grading Standards."

Chapter 2. Helicopters, Lawnmowers, and Stealth Fighters

1. R. Miller, Brady, and Izumi, "Stripping the Wizard's Curtain," 45.

2. Ulferts, "Why Parenting Matters," 11–12.

3. Haller, "What Type of Parent Are You?"

4. Howe, "Meet Mr. and Mrs. Gen X."

5. Lahey, *Gift of Failure*, 31.

6. Ulferts, "Why Parenting Matters," 25.

7. Spera, "Adolescents' Perceptions," 458.

8. R. Miller, Brady, and Izumi, "Stripping the Wizard's Curtain," 47.

9. Mac Iver et al., "Urban Parents at the Portal," 100.

10. Mac Iver et al., "Urban Parents at the Portal," 99.

11. I conducted a personal interview with Cathy on November 3, 2019.

12. Lahey, *Gift of Failure*, 236.

13. Chua, *Battle Hymn of the Tiger Mother*.

14. Levine, *Teach Your Children Well*, 35.

15. Ablard and Parker, "Parents' Achievement Goals and Perfectionism," 652–53.

16. Ablard and Parker, "Parents' Achievement Goals and Perfectionism," 662.

17. Damour, *Under Pressure*, 142–47.

18. Spera, "Adolescents' Perceptions," 486–87.

19. Koplewicz, *Scaffold Effect*, 139.

20. I conducted a personal interview with Erika on February 1, 2023.

21. I conducted a personal interview with DeeDee on February 16, 2023.

22. See Weis and Cippoline, "'Class Work': Producing Privilege," 704–5.

23. National Center for Education Statistics, "Employment and Unemployment Rates by Educational Attainment."

24. Smith and Sun, "Privileged American Families," 159–80.

25. See Korn and Levitz, *Unacceptable*.

26. See, for example, Kahneman and Deaton, "High Income Improves Evaluation of Life but Not Emotional Well-Being," 16489–493.

27. Selingo, *Who Gets In and Why*, 184; 270–71.

28. Liptak, "The Road to a Supreme Court Clerkship."

29. Gray, "As Their Focus on GPA Fades, Employers Seek Key Skills on College Grads' Resumes."

30. Deresiewicz, *Excellent Sheep*.

31. Child Welfare Information Gateway, "What Is Child Abuse and Neglect?"

32. Bright et al., "Friday School Report Card Release," 176–82. The coverage in the *New York Times* was written by Julia Jacobs, "When Report Cards Go Out on Fridays," on December 17, 2018.

33. Toufexis, "Report Cards Can Hurt You."

34. Romeo, "Child Abuse and Report Cards," 438–39.

35. Mandell, "Child Abuse Prevention at Report Card Time."

36. Mandell, "Child Abuse Prevention at Report Card Time," 688.

37. Mandell, "Child Abuse Prevention at Report Card Time," 690.

38. Gopnik, *The Gardener and the Carpenter*, 18–20.

39. Gopnik, *The Gardener and the Carpenter*, 56.

Chapter 3. The Weight of Their World

1. Damour, *Under Pressure*, 138.

2. A useful overview of these categories of stress can be found in Branson, Dry, Palmer, and Turnbull, "Adolescent Distress-Eustress Scale," 1–2. Alpert and Haber developed the now-classic framework for measuring facilitating and debilitating anxiety in "Anxiety in Academic Achievement Situations."

3. For a discussion of the potential benefits of moderate stress, see Henderson, Snyder, Gupta, and Banich, "When Does Stress Help."

4. Shankar and Park, "Effects of Stress on Students' Physical and Mental Health," 6–7.

5. Jones, "Gender-Specific Differences," 739–40.

6. I am indebted to the work of Heather Leslie, particularly her open-access "Executive Summary: Research on Effects of Grading," for drawing my attention to several of the resources that explore the impact of grades on mental health.

7. Sotardi, "Understanding Student Stress and Coping," 714.

8. I conducted a personal interview with Kimberly on February 1 and April 23, 2023.

9. Horowitz and Graf, "Most U.S. Teens See Anxiety and Depression as a Major Problem among Their Peers," 2.

10. Horowitz and Graf, "Most U.S. Teens See Anxiety and Depression as a Major Problem among Their Peers," 9.

11. American College Health Association. "ACHA–National College Health Assessment III," 12.

12. Challenge Success, "Kids under Pressure."

13. These findings are taken verbatim from the CDC fact sheet, "Making the Connection."

14. Reporting on Suicide Collaborative, "Best Practices and Recommendations for Reporting on Suicide."

15. CDC, "Making the Connection," 1.

16. Geiger and Davis, "Growing Number of American Teenagers."

17. Richesson and Hoenig, "Key Substance Use and Mental Health Indicators," 31.

18. Richesson and Hoenig, "Key Substance Use and Mental Health Indicators," 31.

19. Centers for Disease Control and Prevention, "Youth Risk Behavior Survey," 58.

20. Rapaport and Silver, "National Survey Findings."

21. Hibbs and Rostain, *Stressed Years of Their Lives*, 9.

22. The Healthy Minds Network. https://healthymindsnetwork.org/

23. Eisenberg et al., "The Healthy Minds Study: 2021–2022," 3.

24. Eisenberg et al., "The Healthy Minds Study: 2021–2022," 5.

25. Lipson et al., "Trends in College Student Mental Health and Help-Seeking," 138.

26. Office of Special Education and Rehabilitative Services, *Supporting Child and Student Social, Emotional, Behavioral, and Mental Health Needs*, 5–6.

27. Prothero and Riser-Kositsky, "School Counselors and Psychologists Remain Scarce."

28. Prothero and Riser-Kositsky. "School Counselors and Psychologists Remain Scarce."

29. Mollenkamp, "Reeling from the Mental Health Crisis."

30. Barack, "Curriculum a Crucial Component."

31. Modan, "Educators Say They Lack Resources."

32. Office of Special Education and Rehabilitative Services, *Supporting Child and Student Social, Emotional, Behavioral, and Mental Health Needs*, 6 and 83.

33. Abrams, "Student Mental Health Is in Crisis."

34. North Carolina State University's Student Mental Health Task Force, "Report," 4.

35. North Carolina State University's Student Mental Health Task Force, "Report," 6–9.

36. North Carolina State University's Student Mental Health Task Force, "Report," 63–64.

37. Moody, "Multiple Suicides Leave WPI Reeling."

38. Some of this section was originally published in a guest post I wrote on March 7, 2022, for John Warner's "Just Visiting" column in *Inside Higher Ed*.

39. Worcester Polytechnic Institute's Mental Health and Wellbeing Task Force, "Initial Findings and Recommendations."

40. Worcester Polytechnic Institute's Mental Health and Wellbeing Task Force, "Initial Findings and Recommendations," 7.

41. Worcester Polytechnic Institute's Mental Health and Wellbeing Task Force, "Initial Findings and Recommendations," 8.

42. Worcester Polytechnic Institute, "Grade System."

43. Volk, "The Tragedy of Madison Holleran."

44. University of Pennsylvania's Task Force on Student Psychological Health and Welfare, "Report," 2.

45. University of Pennsylvania's Task Force on Student Psychological Health and Welfare, "Report," 4.

46. University of Pennsylvania's Task Force on Student Psychological Health and Welfare, "Report," 6.

47. I conducted a personal interview with Rebecca Bushnell on January 11, 2021.

Chapter 4. Mirror, Mirror, on the Wall

1. "James Meredith's Story."

2. Reece and O'Connell, "Legacy of Slavery," 43.

3. Rooks, *Cutting School*, 12 and 45.

4. Hamilton and Nielsen, *Broke*, 11.

5. Cottom, *Lower Ed*.

6. Rooks, *Cutting School*, 14; Rooks recounts the efforts to end integration on 12–14.

7. Reece and O'Connell, "Legacy of Slavery," 44.

8. Hung et al., "Exploring Student Achievement Gaps," 176.

9. Welner and Carter, "Achievement Gaps," 3.

10. Parks, "Tragedy," n.p.

11. Parks, "Tragedy," n.p.

12. Parks, "Tragedy," n.p.

13. The Big Ten: University of Illinois, Indiana University, University of Iowa, University of Maryland, University of Michigan, Michigan State University, University of Minnesota, University of Nebraska–Lincoln, Northwestern University, Ohio State University, Pennsylvania State University, Purdue University, Rutgers University–New Brunswick, and University of Wisconsin–Madison.

14. See especially Duckworth et al., "Will Not Want" and O'Dea, Lagisz, Jennions, and Nakagawa, "Gender Differences."

15. Riegle-Crumb, "The Path through Math."

16. Herrnstein and Murray, *The Bell Curve*.

17. Gould, *The Mismeasure of Man*, 367–78.

18. Bowen and Cooper, "Grading on a Curve," 188–89.

19. Hogan and Sathy, *Inclusive Teaching*, 80.

20. A. Lewis and Diamond, *Best Intentions*, 14.

21. A. Lewis and Diamond, *Best Intentions*, 12 and 83–118.

22. A. Lewis and Diamond, *Best Intentions*, 10.

23. Calarco, *Negotiating Opportunities*, 161.

24. Calarco, *Negotiating Opportunities*, 161–62.

25. Steele, *Whistling Vivaldi*, 38–40. Steele would later change the parameters of his experiments and remove the issue of performance from the script that he read to the participants. Instead, he focused on the identity being studied independent of performance.

26. Massey and Owens, "Mediators," 559.

27. Massey and Owens, "Mediators," 559.

28. Steele, *Whistling Vivaldi*, 42.

29. Eyler, *How Humans Learn*, 200–201.

30. G. Johnson, "Technology of Surveillance," 54.

31. G. Johnson, "Technology of Surveillance," 56.

32. Bruton and Childers, "Policing Plagiarism," 317–19.

33. Feathers, "Proctorio," n.p.

34. I conducted a personal interview on June 3, 2022. Although I was given permission to use her name, I have retained anonymity to protect the identity of her son.

35. Henry, Catagnus, Griffith, and Garcia, "School-to-Prison Pipeline," n.p.

36. Peguero et al., "School Punishment and Education," 236.

37. Bedi and McGrory, "Pasco's Sheriff," n.p.

Chapter 5. Building Up and Bouncing Back

1. These strategies are taken directly from American Psychological Association, "How to Help Children and Teens Manage Their Stress."

2. Turgeon and Wright, *Generation Sleepless*, 3–4.

3. Lahey, *Addiction Inoculation*, 135.

4. See, for example, McDaniel and Radesky, "Technoference," 100–109.

5. Dweck, *Mindset*, 6–7.

6. Dweck, *Mindset*, 71–73.

7. Dweck, "Praise the Effort, Not the Outcome? Think Again."

8. Dweck, *Mindset*, 32–34.

9. Eyler, *How Humans Learn*, 174–80.

10. Lahey, *Gift of Failure*.

11. Duckworth, *Grit*.

12. Kundu, *Power of Student Agency*, 33–36.

13. Borba, *Thrivers*, 38.

14. Borba, *Thrivers*, 38.

15. Borba, *Thrivers*, 173–78.

16. Eyler, *How Humans Learn*, 29–36.

17. Engel, *The Hungry Mind*, 174–75.

Chapter 6. Reinventing Education

1. Cowan, "Legacy of Grading Contracts, " 2.

2. The essays in Simon and Bellanca, *Degrading*, demonstrate the range of experimentation in the middle of the twentieth century.

3. I conducted a personal interview with Starr Sackstein on April 6, 2022.

4. Sackstein, *Hacking Assessment*.

5. Twitter is unfortunately now known as X, but I remain a conscientious objector to this attempt at rebranding and continue to call the platform Twitter throughout this chapter.

6. I conducted a personal interview with Arthur Chiaravalli on September 19, 2022.

7. Chiaravalli, "Going Gradeless."

8. Doren and Millington, "Pedagogy for Reflective Practice," 75–86.

9. Graham, "Assessment in the Visual Arts," 175–83.

10. Yancey, "Looking Back, " 499.

11. Fields et al., "Communicating about Computational Thinking," 1–35.

12. D. Lewis, "Impacts," 67.

13. Clark and Talbert, *Grading for Growth*, 158.

14. D. Lewis, "Impacts," 68.

15. Naramore and Frangiosa, *Going Gradeless*, 62.

16. See Nilson, *Specifications Grading*.

17. Grau, "'Streamlined' Contract Grading," 255.

18. Used with permission from Sue Ann Skipworth's syllabus for Political Science 101: "Introduction to American Politics" (Spring 2022).

19. Danielewicz and Elbow, "A Unilateral Grading Contract," 246.

20. Inoue, *Labor-Based Grading Contracts*, 126–32.

21. Filene, "Self-Grading," 451–58.

22. Blum, *Ungrading*, incorporates all three of these definitions throughout.

23. See Masland, "Ungrading," 89; and Dyer's Twitter thread from May 6, 2022: https://twitter.com/YouTooBio/status/1522678959359549442

24. Stommel, "Ungrading."

25. I conducted a personal interview with Courtney Sobers on April 8, 2022.

26. I conducted a personal interview with Nick Covington on August 31, 2022.

27. See Guberman, "Student Perceptions," 91–95.

28. Feldman, *Grading for Equity*, 89.

29. D. Lewis, "Impacts," 67.

30. The Grading Conference. https://thegradingconference.com/

Chapter 7. Climbing Mountains

1. Gannon, *Radical Hope*, 5.

2. David M. Perry's CNN article "Why a Pass/Fail Option Is a Good Move for All," published very early in the pandemic, provides an important snapshot of the early phase of this temporary shift in grading policies. Around the same time, Laura Gibbs, formerly of the University of Oklahoma, began recording information about universities that were making changes to their grading models in a publicly available spreadsheet: "#PassFailNation: Alternate Grading."

3. See, for example, Anderson, "Harvard."

4. Evergreen State College, "Student Body Fall 2023."

5. More information about Evergreen's evaluation system is available on the college's website: https://www.evergreen.edu/evaluations.

6. Here and elsewhere, comments from Brad Proctor come from a personal interview on August 24, 2021.

7. Here and elsewhere, comments from Pauline Yu come from a personal interview on September 10, 2021.

8. Here and elsewhere, comments from Stacey Davis come from a personal interview on August 24, 2021.

9. I conducted a personal interview with Krishna Chowdary on August 24, 2021.

10. Evergreen State College Office of Institutional Research and Assessment, "The Evergreen State College Five/Ten/Fifteen-Year Alumni Survey," 17–36. In this same vein, New College of Florida—another public, gradeless college—was able to boast as recently as 2023 that it was the top institution in the country in terms of "producing the highest percentage of undergraduates who go on to earn PhDs in science and engineering." See New College of Florida, "Outcomes of Graduates."

11. https://www.evergreen.edu/evaluations

12. I conducted a personal interview with David McAvity on January 24, 2022.

13. https://seventh.ucsd.edu/about/prospective-students/index.html

14. Here and elsewhere, comments from Jill Gladstein come from a personal interview on January 25, 2022.

15. Burke, "Ditching Letter-Grade System."

16. LD 1422. The bill was introduced in 2011, and the law was passed in 2012. http://www.mainelegislature.org/legis/bills/bills_125th /billtexts/SP043901.asp

17. https://education.vermont.gov/student-learning/flexible-pathways

18. https://legislature.vermont.gov/bill/status/2022/H.181

19. Barnum, "Maine Went All In." Issues about equity were raised in K. Miller, "Legislators Vote."

20. A. Johnson, *Maine's Superintendents' Perceptions*, 2.

21. https://education.vermont.gov/sites/aoe/files/documents/edu -vermont-proficiency-based-grading-practices.pdf

22. Many of these resources can be found on this website: https:// education.vermont.gov/student-learning/proficiency-based -learning#grading-practices, and the glossary of terms can be found here: https://education.vermont.gov/sites/aoe/files/documents/edu -proficiency-based-learning-glossary_0.pdf

23. A. Johnson, *Maine's Superintendents' Perceptions*, 2.

24. https://education.vermont.gov/sites/aoe/files/documents/edu -proficiency-based-grading-and-transcripts-responding-to-parent -and-community-concerns.pdf

25. Cover, "Frustrated Maine Parents."

26. https://www.epcusd401.org/about/basic-info

27. Here and elsewhere, comments from Leah Gauthier come from a personal interview on September 10, 2021.

28. Pollard, "Santa Fe Public Schools."

29. The information guide on their website can be found here: https://go .lindberghschools.ws/Page/16299.

30. Guskey, "Learning from Failures," 192–99. Guskey's framework is certainly not the only model for educational reform, but it is one of the few to focus predominantly on grading.

31. Guskey, "Learning from Failures," 196.

32. Guskey, "Learning from Failures," 196.

33. This data has been compiled by the National Center for Education Statistics, "Fast Facts: Homeschooling."

34. A 2021 study by the National Home Education Research Institute reports this higher number of homeschooled children just prior to the pandemic: https://www.nheri.org/how-many-homeschool-students -are-there-in-the-united-states-pre-covid-19-and-post-covid-19/. Tate, "Colleges Welcome," cites similar data regarding numbers of home-schoolers but also discusses their success with getting into college.

35. I conducted a personal interview with James Corner on February 10, 2021.

36. I conducted a personal interview with this director on January 18, 2022.

37. See Selingo, *Who Gets In and Why*, esp. 104–5.

38. John Tagg in his book *The Instruction Myth* identifies community as a key element of reform initiatives in higher education (10).

Bibliography

Ablard, Karen E., and Wayne D. Parker. "Parents' Achievement Goals and Perfectionism in Their Academically Talented Children." *Journal of Youth and Adolescence* 26.6 (1997): 651–67.

Abrams, Zara. "Student Mental Health Is in Crisis: Campuses Are Rethinking Their Approach." *Monitor on Psychology* 53 (October 12, 2022): n.p. https://www.apa.org/monitor/2022/10/mental-health-campus-care

Alpert, Richard, and Ralph Norman Haber. "Anxiety in Academic Achievement Situations." *Journal of Abnormal and Social Psychology* 61 (1960): 207–15.

American College Health Association. "ACHA–National College Health Assessment III: Undergraduate Student Reference Group Executive Summary, Fall 2022." Silver Spring, MD: American College Health Association, 2023. 1–23. https://www.acha.org/documents/ncha/NCHA-III_FALL_2022_UNDERGRADUATE_REFERENCE_GROUP_EXECUTIVE_SUMMARY.pdf

American Montessori Society. "Montessori FAQs." https://amshq.org/Families/Why-Choose-Montessori/Montessori-FAQs#givegrades

American Psychological Association. "How to Help Children and Teens Manage Their Stress." October 19, 2022. https://www.apa.org/topics/children/stress

Anderman, Eric M., and Alison C. Koenka. "The Relation between Academic Motivation and Cheating." *Theory into Practice* 56 (2017): 95–102.

Anderson, Nick. "Harvard Won't Require SAT or ACT through 2026 as Test-Optional Push Grows." *Washington Post*, December 16, 2021. https://www.washingtonpost.com/education/2021/12/16/harvard-test-optional-college-admissions

Bain, Ken. *What the Best College Teachers Do*. Cambridge, MA: Harvard University Press, 2004.

Bar, Talia, Vrinda Kadiyali, and Asaf Zussman. "Grade Information and Grade Inflation: The Cornell Experiment." *Journal of Economic Perspectives* 23.3 (2009): 93–108.

Barack, Lauren. "Curriculum a Crucial Component of School Mental Health Strategies." *K–12 Dive*, September 7, 2022. https://www.k12dive.com/news/curriculum-a-crucial-component-of-school-mental-health-approaches/631346/

Barnum, Matt. "Maine Went All in on 'Proficiency-Based Learning'—then Rolled It Back. What Does That Mean for the Rest of the Country?" *Chalkbeat*, October 18, 2018. https://www.chalkbeat.org/2018/10/18/21105950/maine-went-all-in-on-proficiency-based-learning-then-rolled-it-back-what-does-that-mean-for-the-rest

Bedi, Neil, and Kathleen McGrory. "Pasco's Sheriff Uses Grades and Abuse Histories to Label Schoolchildren Potential Criminals: The Kids and Their Parents Don't Know." *Tampa Bay Times*, November 19, 2020. https://projects.tampabay.com/projects/2020/investigations/police-pasco-sheriff-targeted/school-data/#:~:text=The%20Pasco%20Sheriff's%20Office%20uses,at%20risk%20of%20becoming%20criminals

Big Ten Academic Alliance. https://btaa.org/about

Blum, Susan D. "Introduction: Why Ungrade? Why Grade?" In *Ungrading: Why Rating Students Undermines Learning (and What to Do Instead)*. Ed. Susan D. Blum. Morgantown: West Virginia University Press, 2020. 1–22.

Blum, Susan D., ed. *Ungrading: Why Rating Students Undermines Learning (and What to Do Instead)*. Morgantown: West Virginia University Press, 2020.

Borba, Michele. *Thrivers: The Surprising Reasons Why Some Kids Struggle and Others Shine*. New York: Putnam, 2021.

Bowen, Ryan S., and Melanie M. Cooper. "Grading on a Curve as a Systemic Issue of Equity in Chemistry Education." *Journal of Chemical Education* 99 (2022): 185–95.

Branson, Victoria, Matthew J. Dry, Edward Palmer, and Deborah Turnbull. "The Adolescent Distress-Eustress Scale: Development and Validation." *SAGE Open* 9.3 (2019): 1–14.

Bright, Melissa, et al. "Association of Friday School Report Card Release with Saturday Incidence Rates of Agency-Verified Physical Child

Abuse." *Journal of the American Medical Association Pediatrics* 173 (2019): 176–82.

Brookhart, Susan M., et. al. "A Century of Grading Research: Meaning and Value in the Most Common Educational Measure." *Review of Educational Research* 86 (2016): 803–48.

Bruton, Samuel, and Dan Childers. "The Ethics and Politics of Policing Plagiarism: A Qualitative Study of Faculty Views on Student Plagiarism and Turnitin." *Assessment & Evaluation in Higher Education* 41 (2016): 316–30.

Burke, Michael. "University of California Departments Consider Ditching Letter-Grade System for New Students." *KQED*, April 26, 2022. https://www.kqed.org/news/11912248/university-of-california-departments-consider-ditching-letter-grade-system-for-new-students

Butler, Ruth, and Mordecai Nisan. "Effects of No Feedback, Task-Related Comments, and Grades on Intrinsic Motivation and Performance." *Journal of Educational Psychology* 78 (1986): 210–16.

Calarco, Jessica McCrory. *Negotiating Opportunities: How the Middle Class Secures Advantages in School.* New York: Oxford University Press, 2018.

Campbell, Corbin M., and Alberto F. Cabrera. "Making the Mark: Are Grades and Deep Learning Related?" *Research in Higher Education* 55.5 (2014): 494–507.

Centers for Disease Control and Prevention. "Making the Connection: Suicidal Thoughts and Behaviors and Academic Grades." Department of Health and Human Services, 2016. https://www.cdc.gov/healthyyouth/health_and_academics/pdf/DASHfactsheetSuicidal.pdf

———. "Youth Risk Behavior Survey: Data Summary & Trends Report, 2011–2021." Department of Health and Human Services, April 2023. https://www.cdc.gov/healthyyouth/data/yrbs/pdf/YRBS_Data-Summary-Trends_Report2023_508.pdf

Cerasoli, Christopher P., Jessica M. Nicklin, and Michael T. Ford. "Intrinsic Motivation and Extrinsic Incentives Jointly Predict Performance: A 40-Year Meta-Analysis." *Psychological Bulletin* 140.4 (2014): 980–1008.

Challenge Success. "Kids under Pressure." Challenge Success–NBC News, February 2021. https://challengesuccess.org/wp-content/uploads/2021/02/CS-NBC-Study-Kids-Under-Pressure-PUBLISHED.pdf

Chiaravalli, Arthur. "Why Teachers Are Going Gradeless." *New York Observer*, April 13, 2017. https://observer.com/2017/04/teachers-going-gradeless-education-reform-grades/

Child Welfare Information Gateway. "What Is Child Abuse and Neglect? Recognizing the Signs and Symptoms." Washington, DC: US Department of Health and Human Services, Children's Bureau, 2019. https://www.childwelfare.gov/pubpdfs/whatiscan.pdf

Chua, Amy. *Battle Hymn of the Tiger Mother*. New York: Penguin, 2011.

Clark, David, and Robert Talbert. *Grading for Growth: A Guide to Alternative Grading Practices that Promote Authentic Learning and Student Engagement in Higher Education*. New York: Routledge, 2023.

Clune, Michael W. "AI Means Professors Need to Raise Their Grading Standards." *Chronicle of Higher Education*, September 12, 2023.

Cottom, Tressie McMillan. *Lower Ed: The Troubling Rise of For-Profit Colleges in the New Economy*. New York: New Press, 2017.

Cover, Susan. "Frustrated Maine Parents Rally against Proficiency-Based Learning." *The Maine Monitor*, April 6, 2018. https://www.themainemonitor.org/frustrated-maine-parents-rally-against-proficiency-based-learning/

Cowan, Michelle. "A Legacy of Grading Contracts for Composition." *Journal of Writing Assessment* 13.2 (2020): 1–16.

Crocker, Jennifer, Andrew Karpinski, Diane M. Quinn, and Sara K. Chase. "What Grades Determine Self-Worth: Consequences of Contingent Self-Worth for Male and Female Engineering and Psychology Majors." *Journal of Personality and Social Psychology* 85 (2003): 507–16.

Crocker, Jennifer, Riia K. Luhtanen, M. Lynne Cooper, and Alexandra Bouvrette. "Contingencies of Self-Worth in College Students: Theory and Measurement." *Journal of Personality and Social Psychology* 85 (2003): 894–908.

Damour, Lisa. *Under Pressure: Confronting the Epidemic of Stress and Anxiety in Girls*. New York: Ballantine, 2019.

Danielewicz, Jane, and Peter Elbow. "A Unilateral Grading Contract to Improve Learning and Teaching." *College Composition and Communication* 61 (2009): 244–68.

Davidson, Cathy. *The New Education: How to Revolutionize the University to Prepare Students for a World in Flux*. New York: Basic, 2017.

Deci, Edward L., with Richard Flaste. *Why We Do What We Do: Understanding Self-Motivation*. New York: Penguin, 1995.

Deresiewicz, William. *Excellent Sheep: The Miseducation of the American Elite and the Way to a Meaningful Life*. New York: Free Press, 2014.

Doren, Mariah, and Anette Millington. "A Pedagogy for Reflective Practice: Art and Design Thinking Made Visible Using and Online Learning Portfolio." *International Journal of ePortfolio* 9 (2019): 75–86.

Duckworth, Angela. *Grit: The Power of Passion and Perseverance.* New York: Scribner, 2016.

Duckworth, Angela L., et al. "Will Not Want: Self-Control Rather than Motivation Explains the Female Advantage in Report Card Grades." *Learning and Individual Differences* 39 (2015): 13–23.

Dweck, Carol. *Mindset: The New Psychology of Success.* New York: Ballantine, 2006.

———. "Praise the Effort, Not the Outcome? Think Again." *Times Educational Supplement*, January 31, 2016. https://www.tes.com/magazine /archive/praise-effort-not-outcome-think-again

Eisenberg, Daniel, et al. "The Healthy Minds Study: 2021–2022 Data Report." Healthy Minds Network, 2023. 1–12. https:// healthymindsnetwork.org/wp-content/uploads/2023/03/HMS_na tional_print-6-1.pdf

Elmwood Park Community Unit School District #401. "Basic Info." https://www.epcusd401.org/about/basic-info

Engel, Susan. *The Hungry Mind: The Origins of Curiosity in Childhood.* Cambridge, MA: Harvard University Press, 2015.

Evergreen State College. "Narrative Evaluations." https://www.evergreen .edu/evaluations

———. "Student Body Fall 2023." https://www.evergreen.edu/sites/default /files/2023-10/EnrollmentOverview_Fall2023_0.pdf

Evergreen State College Office of Institutional Research and Assessment. "The Evergreen State College Five/Ten/Fifteen-Year Alumni Survey: Administered to the Undergraduate Classes of 2012, 2007, and 2002 in 2017." January 2018. 1–76. https://www.evergreen.edu/sites/default /files/2023-07/5_10_15-Year%20Alumni%20Survey%202017.pdf

Eyler, Joshua R. "Grades Are at the Center of the Student Mental Health Crisis." *Inside Higher Ed*, March 7, 2022. https://www.insidehighered .com/blogs/just-visiting/grades-are-center-student-mental-health -crisis

———. *How Humans Learn: The Science and Stories behind Effective College Teaching.* Morgantown: West Virginia University Press, 2018.

Feathers, Todd. "Proctorio Is Using Racist Algorithms to Detect Faces." *Vice*, April 8, 2021. https://www.vice.com/en/article/g5gxg3/proctorio -is-using-racist-algorithms-to-detect-faces

Feldman, Joe. *Grading for Equity: What It Is, Why It Matters, and How It Can Transform Schools and Classrooms*. Thousand Oaks, CA: Corwin, 2019.

Fields, Deborah, et al. "Communicating about Computational Thinking: Understanding Affordances of Portfolios for Assessing High School Students' Computational Thinking and Participation Practices." *Computer Science Education* (2021): 1–35.

Filene, Peter. "Self-Grading: An Experiment in Learning." *Journal of Higher Education* 40 (1969): 451–58.

Gannon, Kevin. *Radical Hope: A Teaching Manifesto*. Morgantown: West Virginia University Press, 2020.

Geiger, A. W., and Leslie Davis. "A Growing Number of American Teen-agers—Particularly Girls—Are Facing Depression." Pew Research Center, July 12, 2019. https://www.pewresearch.org/fact-tank/2019/07/12/a-growing-number-of-american-teenagers-particularly-girls-are-facing-depression

Gibbs, Laura. "#PassFailNation: Alternate Grading." *OU Digital Teaching* (blog). https://oudigitools.blogspot.com/2020/03/feedback-alternate-grading-in-crisis.html

Gopnik, Alison. *The Gardener and the Carpenter: What the New Science of Child Development Tells Us about the Relationship between Parents and Children*. New York: Picador, 2016.

Gould, Stephen Jay. *The Mismeasure of Man*. Revised and expanded ed. New York: Norton, 1996.

Graham, Mark. "Assessment in the Visual Arts: Challenges and Possibilities." *Arts Education Policy Review* 120.3 (2019): 175–83.

Grau, Harold J. "'Streamlined' Contract Grading—A Performance-Measuring Alternative to Traditional Evaluation Methods." *Journal of College Science Teaching* 28.4 (1999): 254–58.

Gray, Kevin. "As Their Focus on GPA Fades, Employers Seek Key Skills on College Grads' Resumes." National Association of Colleges and Employers, November 15, 2022. https://www.naceweb.org/talent-acquisition/candidate-selection/as-their-focus-on-gpa-fades-employers-seek-key-skills-on-college-grads-resumes/

Guberman, Daniel. "Student Perceptions of an Online Ungraded Course." *Teaching and Learning Inquiry* 9 (2021): 86–98.

Guskey, Thomas. "Learning from Failures: Lessons from Unsuccessful Grading Reform Initiatives." *NASSP Bulletin* 105 (2021): 192–99.

Haller, Sonja. "What Type of Parent Are You? Lawnmower? Helicopter? Attachment? Tiger? Free-range?" *USA Today*, September 19, 2018. https://www.usatoday.com/story/life/allthemoms/2018/09/19 /parenting-terms-explained-lawnmower-helicopter-attachment-tiger -free-range-dolphin-elephant/1357612002/

Hamilton, Laura T., and Kelly Nielsen. *Broke: The Racial Consequences of Underfunding Public Universities*. Chicago: University of Chicago Press, 2021.

Hawthorne, Nathaniel. *The Scarlet Letter*. Eds. Seymour Gross et al. 3rd ed. New York: Norton, 1988.

Henderson, Roselinde K., Hannah R. Snyder, Tina Gupta, and Marie T. Banich. "When Does Stress Help or Harm? The Effects of Stress Controllability and Subjective Stress Response on Stroop Performance." *Frontiers in Psychology* 3 (2012): 1–15.

Henry, Kade-Ann K., Robyn M. Catagnus, Annette K. Griffith, and Yors A. Garcia. "Ending the School-to-Prison Pipeline: Perception and Experience with Zero-Tolerance Policies and Interventions to Address Racial Inequality." *Behavior Analysis in Practice* (2021): online only, n.p.

Herrnstein, Richard J., and Charles Murray. *The Bell Curve: Intelligence and Class Structure in American Life*. New York: Free Press, 1994.

Hibbs, B. Janet, and Anthony Rostain. *The Stressed Years of Their Lives: Helping Your Kid Survive and Thrive during Their College Years*. New York: St. Martin's, 2019.

Hogan, Kelly A., and Viji Sathy. *Inclusive Teaching: Strategies for Promoting Equity in the College Classroom*. Morgantown: West Virginia University Press, 2022.

Holland, Mary N. "Creating Effective Pupil Reports." *Bulletin of the Department of Elementary School Principals* 10 (1931): 363–72.

Horowitz, Juliana Menasce, and Nikki Graf. "Most U.S. Teens See Anxiety and Depression as a Major Problem among Their Peers." Pew Research Center, February 20, 2019. https://www.pewresearch.org/social-trends /wp-content/uploads/sites/3/2019/02/Pew-Research-Center_Teens -report_full-2.pdf

Howe, Neil. "Meet Mr. and Mrs. Gen X: A New Parent Generation." *School Administrator Magazine*, January 20, 2010. http://www.aasa .org/resources/resource/meet-mr-and-mrs-gen-x-a-new-parent -generation

Hung, Man, et al. "Exploring Student Achievement Gaps in School Districts across the United States." *Education and Urban Society* 52.2 (2020): 175–93.

Inoue, Asao. *Labor-Based Grading Contracts: Building Equity and Inclusion in the Compassionate Writing Classroom.* 2nd ed. Denver: University Press of Colorado, 2022.

Jacobs, Julia. "When Report Cards Go Out on Fridays, Child Abuse Increases on Saturdays, Study Finds." *New York Times*, December 17, 2018. https://www.nytimes.com/2018/12/17/health/child-abuse-report -cards-florida.html

"James Meredith's Story." University of Mississippi. https://60years.olemiss .edu/your-stories/james-meredith/

Johnson, Amy F. *Maine's Superintendents' Perceptions of Proficiency-based Education and Proficiency-based Diploma Systems.* Gorham, ME: Maine Education Policy Research Institute at the University of Southern Maine, 2019. https://digitalcommons.usm.maine.edu/cgi/viewcont ent.cgi?article=1015&context=cepare_state

Johnson, Gavin P. "Grades as a Technology of Surveillance: Normalization, Control, and Big Data in the Teaching of Writing." In *Privacy Matters: Conversations about Surveillance Within and Beyond the Classroom.* Eds. Estee Beck and Les Hutchinson Campos. Logan: Utah State University Press, 2021. 53–72.

Johnson, Valen E. *Grade Inflation: A Crisis in College Education.* Springer Science & Business Media, 2006.

Jones, Russell W. "Gender-Specific Differences in the Perceived Antecedents of Academic Stress." *Psychological Reports* 72 (1993): 739–43.

Kahneman, Daniel, and Angus Deaton. "High Income Improves Evaluation of Life but not Emotional Well-Being." *Proceedings of the National Academy of Sciences* 107.38 (2010): 16489–493.

Kane, John, and Rebecca Mushtare, hosts. "Takeover: Sarah Cavanagh and Josh Eyler Interview Each Other." *Tea for Teaching* (podcast), October 14, 2020. https://www.podbean.com/media/share/pb-zxcb4-ef45bf ?utm_campaign=au_share_ep&utm_medium=dlink&utm_source=au _share

Koenka, Alison C., et al. "A Meta-Analysis on the Impact of Grades and Comments on Academic Motivation and Achievement: A Case for Written Feedback." *Educational Psychology* 41.7 (2021): 922–47.

Kohn, Alfie. "The Dangerous Myth of Grade Inflation." *Chronicle of Higher Education*, November 8, 2002.

———. *Punished by Rewards: The Trouble with Gold Stars, Incentive Plans, A's, Praise, and Other Bribes*. New York: Houghton Mifflin, 1993.

Koplewicz, Harold S. *The Scaffold Effect: Raising Resilient, Self-Reliant, and Secure Kids in an Age of Anxiety*. New York: Harmony, 2021.

Korn, Melissa, and Jennifer Levitz. *Unacceptable: Privilege, Deceit, and the Making of the College Admissions Scandal*. New York: Portfolio/ Penguin, 2020.

Kundu, Anindya. *The Power of Student Agency: Looking beyond Grit to Close the Opportunity Gap*. New York: Teachers College Press, 2020.

Lahey, Jessica. *The Addiction Inoculation: Raising Healthy Kids in a Culture of Dependence*. New York: HarperCollins, 2021.

———. *The Gift of Failure: How the Best Parents Learn to Let Go so Their Children Can Succeed*. New York: HarperCollins, 2015.

Lamott, Anne. *Bird by Bird: Some Instructions on Writing and Life*. New York: Anchor, 1995.

Lang, James M. *Cheating Lessons: Learning from Academic Dishonesty*. Cambridge, MA: Harvard UP, 2013.

Leslie, Heather. "Executive Summary: Research on Effects of Grading." Open-access online resource. https://docs.google.com/file/d/1ssxxIkuur 6mwovObQQZHC5yd0vgDvNOx/edit?filetype=msword

Levine, Madeline. *Teach Your Children Well: Why Values and Coping Skills Matter More than Grades, Trophies, or "Fat Envelopes."* New York: HarperCollins, 2012.

Lewis, Amanda E., and John B. Diamond. *Despite the Best Intentions: How Racial Inequality Thrives in Good Schools*. New York: Oxford University Press, 2015.

Lewis, Drew. "Impacts of Standards-Based Grading on Students' Mindset and Test Anxiety." *Journal of the Scholarship of Teaching and Learning* 22.2 (2022): 67–77.

Lindbergh Schools. "District Grading Practices." YouTube video. https:// www.youtube.com/watch?v=DdpL2R_vnjE&feature=youtube

———. "Standards-Based Learning." Online resource. https://go.lindbergh schools.ws/Page/16299

Lipson, Sarah Ketchen, et al. "Trends in College Student Mental Health and Help-Seeking by Race/Ethnicity: Findings from the National Healthy Minds Study, 2013–2021." *Journal of Affective Disorders* 306 (2022): 138–47.

Liptak, Adam. "The Road to a Supreme Court Clerkship Starts at Three Ivy League Colleges." *New York Times*, February 6, 2023. https://www

.nytimes.com/2023/02/06/us/supreme-court-ivy-league-harvard-yale
.html

Love, Bettina L. *We Want to Do More than Survive: Abolitionist Teaching and the Pursuit of Educational Freedom*. Boston: Beacon, 2019.

Mac Iver, Martha Abele, et al. "Urban Parents at the Portal: Family Use of Web-Based Information on Ninth Grade Student Course Grades." *School Community Journal* 31 (2021): 85–108.

Maine Legislature. LD 1422: "An Act to Prepare Maine People for the Future Economy." 2011. http://www.mainelegislature.org/legis/bills /bills_125th/billtexts/SP043901.asp

Mandell, Sara. "Child Abuse Prevention at Report Card Time." *Journal of Community Psychology* 28.6 (2000): 687–90.

Mann, Horace. *Lectures on Education*. New York: Arno, 1969. First published 1855 by Ide & Dutton.

———. *Ninth Annual Report of the Secretary of the Board of Education*. Boston: Dutton and Wentworth, 1846. Retrieved from Archives of the State Library of Massachusetts. https://archives.lib.state.ma.us/handle /2452/204728

———. *Seventh Annual Report of the Secretary of the Board of Education*. Boston: Dutton and Wentworth, 1844. Retrieved from Archives of the State Library of Massachusetts. Archives of the State Library of Massachusetts. https://archives.lib.state.ma.us/handle/2452/204726

———. *Tenth Annual Report of the Secretary of the Board of Education*. Boston: Dutton and Wentworth, 1847. Retrieved from Archives of the State Library of Massachusetts. https://archives.lib.state.ma.us/handle /2452/204729

Masland, Lindsay. "Ungrading: The Joys of Doing Everything Wrong." *Zeal: A Journal for the Liberal Arts* 1 (2023): 88–93.

Massey, Douglas S., and Jayanti Owens. "Mediators of Stereotype Threat among Black College Students." *Ethnic and Racial Studies* 37 (2014): 557–75.

McDaniel, Brandon T., and Jenny S. Radesky. "Technoference: Parent Distraction with Technology and Associations with Child Behavior Problems." *Child Development* 89 (2018): 100–109.

Michaels, Kate, and Jocelyn Milner. "Powered by Publics Learning Memo: The Big Ten Academic Alliance Cluster Exploring Foundational Course DFW Rates, Equity Gaps, and Progress to Degree." Association of Public and Land-grant Universities, 2021. https://www.aplu.org

/library/powered-by-publics-learning-memo-the-big-ten-academic
-alliance-cluster/file

Miller, Kevin. "Legislators Vote to Ease Maine's Proficiency-Based Education Mandate, Allow More 'Local Control.'" *Press Herald*, June 28, 2018. https://www.pressherald.com/2018/06/27/lawmakers-vote-to
-eliminate-proficiency-based-education-mandate-in-maine/

Miller, Roxanne Greitz, John T. Brady, and Jared T. Izumi. "Stripping the Wizard's Curtain: Examining the Practice of Online Grade Booking in K–12 Schools." *School Community Journal* 26.2 (2016): 45–69.

Modan, Naaz. "Educators Say They Lack Resources to Address Worsening Mental Health Crisis." *K–12 Dive*, February 16, 2023. https://www
.k12dive.com/news/superintendents-teachers-resources-student
-mental-health_crisis/642940/

Mollenkamp, Daniel. "Reeling from the Mental Health Crisis, K–12 Districts Turn to Telemedicine." *EdSurge*, February 6, 2023. https://
www.edsurge.com/news/2023-02-06-reeling-from-the-mental-health
-crisis-k-12-districts-turn-to-telemedicine

Moody, Josh. "Multiple Suicides Leave WPI Reeling." *Inside Higher Ed*, February 2, 2022. https://www.insidehighered.com/news/2022/02/03
/multiple-suicides-leave-wpi-reeling

Morris, Wade H. *Report Cards: A Cultural History*. Baltimore: Johns Hopkins University Press, 2023.

Naramore, Elise B., and David K. Frangiosa. *Going Gradeless, Grades 6–12: Shifting the Focus to Student Learning*. Thousand Oaks, CA: Corwin, 2021.

National Center for Education Statistics. "Employment and Unemployment Rates by Educational Attainment." US Department of Education, Institute of Education Sciences, May 2022. https://nces.ed.gov
/programs/coe/indicator/cbc/employment-unemployment-rates
———. "Fast Facts: Homeschooling." US Department of Education, Institute of Education Sciences, 2021. https://nces.ed.gov/fastfacts
/display.asp?id=91

National Center for Montessori in the Public Sector. "About Montessori." https://www.public-montessori.org/montessori/#:~:text=There%20
about%2020%2C000%20Montessori%20schools,district%2C%20
magnet%2C%20and%20charters

National Home Education Research Institute. "How Many Homeschool Students Are There in the United States? Pre-Covid-19 and

Post-Covid-19: New Data." September 9, 2021. https://www.nheri.org
/how-many-homeschool-students-are-there-in-the-united-states-pre
-covid-19-and-post-covid-19/

New College of Florida. "Outcomes of Graduates." https://www.ncf.edu
/admissions/outcomes-of-graduates/

Nilson, Linda B. *Specifications Grading: Restoring Rigor, Motivating
Students, and Saving Faculty Time*. Sterling, VA: Stylus, 2014.

North Carolina State University's Student Mental Health Task Force.
"Report." February 2023. 1–89. https://drive.google.com/file/d/1Ous6c
YHh9yJtJOUti7We4nGPxvfXTs5X/view

O'Dea, Rose E., Malgorzata Lagisz, Michael D. Jennions, and Shinichi
Nakagawa. "Gender Differences in Individual Variation in Academic
Grades Fail to Fit Expected Patterns for STEM." *Nature Communica-
tions* 9 (2018): 1–8.

Office of Special Education and Rehabilitative Services. *Supporting Child
and Student Social, Emotional, Behavioral, and Mental Health Needs*.
US Department of Education, 2021. 1–103. https://www2.ed.gov
/documents/students/supporting-child-student-social-emotional
-behavioral-mental-health.pdf

Office of the US Surgeon General. *Protecting Youth Mental Health: The US
Surgeon General's Advisory*. Department of Health and Human
Services, December 6, 2021. https://www.hhs.gov/sites/default/files
/surgeon-general-youth-mental-health-advisory.pdf

Parks, Casey. "The Tragedy of America's Rural Schools." *New York Times
Magazine*, September 9, 2021. https://www.nytimes.com/2021/09/07
/magazine/rural-public-education.html

Peguero, Anthony A., et al. "School Punishment and Education: Racial/
Ethnic Disparities with Grade Retention and the Role of Urbanicity."
Urban Education 56 (2021): 228–60.

Perry, David M. "Why a Pass/Fail Option Is a Good Move for All." *CNN*,
March 18, 2020. https://www.cnn.com/2020/03/18/opinions
/coronavirus-makes-college-and-life-pass-fail-perry/

Pollard, Jessica. "Santa Fe Public Schools Prepares to Dramatically Change
Grading." *Santa Fe New Mexican*, January 31, 2022. https://www
.santafenewmexican.com/news/education/santa-fe-public-schools
-prepares-to-dramatically-change-grading/article_21f2a9de-5174-11ec
-9596-3b273b51e244.html

Prothero, Arianna, and Maya Riser-Kositsky. "School Counselors and
Psychologists Remain Scarce Even as Needs Rise." *Education Week*,

March 1, 2022. https://www.edweek.org/leadership/school-counselors
-and-psychologists-remain-scarce-even-as-needs-rise/2022/03

Pulfrey, Caroline, Céline Buchs, and Fabrizio Butera. "Why Grades
Engender Performance-Avoidance Goals: The Mediating Role of
Autonomous Motivation." *Journal of Educational Psychology* 103.3
(2011): 683–700.

Quinn, Ryan. "At Michigan, Getting an A because Your Instructor's on
Strike." *Inside Higher Ed*, May 19, 2023. https://www.insidehighered
.com/news/faculty-issues/labor-unionization/2023/05/19/michigan
-getting-because-your-instructors-strike

Rapaport, Amie, and Daniel Silver. "National Survey Findings Shed Light
on Dimensions of Teen Mental Health Concerns." University of Southern California's Dornsife Center for Economic and Social Research,
November 11, 2022. https://healthpolicy.usc.edu/evidence-base
/national-survey-findings-shed-light-on-dimensions-of-teen-mental
-health-concerns/

Reece, Robert L., and Heather A. O'Connell. "How the Legacy of Slavery
and Racial Composition Shape Public School Enrollment in the
American South." *Sociology of Race and Ethnicity* 2 (2016): 42–57.

Reporting on Suicide Collaborative. "Best Practices and Recommendations
for Reporting on Suicide." Suicide Awareness Voices of Education (SAVE),
2020. https://reportingonsuicide.org/recommendations/#dodonts

Richesson, Douglas, and Jennifer M. Hoenig. *Key Substance Use and
Mental Health Indicators in the United States: Results from the 2020
National Survey on Drug Use and Health.* Substance Abuse and Mental
Health Services Administration, Department of Health and Human
Services, October 2021. 1–156. https://www.samhsa.gov/data/sites
/default/files/reports/rpt35325/NSDUHFFRPDFWHTMLFiles2020
/2020NSDUHFFR1PDFW102121.pdf

Riegle-Crumb, Catherine. "The Path through Math: Course Sequences and
Academic Performance at the Intersection of Race-Ethnicity and
Gender." *American Journal of Education* 113 (2006): 101–22.

Romeo, Felicia F. "Child Abuse and Report Cards." *Education* 120.3
(2000): 438–41.

Rooks, Noliwe. *Cutting School: The Segrenomics of American Education.*
New York: New Press, 2017.

Ross, Jennifer, et al. "Teaching Report: Instructor Perspectives on Failure
and Its Role in Learning in Higher Education." *Currents in Teaching
and Learning* 14 (2023): 83–102.

Ryan, Richard M., and Edward L. Deci. "Intrinsic and Extrinsic Motivation from a Self-Determination Theory Perspective: Definitions, Theory, Practices, and Future Directions." *Contemporary Educational Psychology* 61 (2020): 1–11.

Sackstein, Starr. *Hacking Assessment: 10 Ways to Go Gradeless in a Traditional Grades School.* 2nd ed. Cleveland: Times 10, 2022.

Schneider, Jack, and Ethan Hutt. "Making the Grade: A History of the A–F Marking Scheme." *Journal of Curriculum Studies* 46 (2014): 201–24.

Selingo, Jeffrey. *Who Gets In and Why: A Year inside College Admissions.* New York: Scribner, 2020.

Shankar, Nilani L., and Crystal L. Park. "Effects of Stress on Students' Physical and Mental Health and Academic Success." *International Journal of School and Educational Psychology* 4 (2016): 5–9.

Simon, Sidney B., and James A. Bellanca. *Degrading the Grading Myths: A Primer of Alternatives to Grades and Marks.* Washington, DC: Association for Supervision and Curriculum Development, 1976.

Singh, Sunil. "Grading Gets an F: A Mathematician's Guide to the Absurdity of Numerical Assessment." *Human Restoration Project*, December 6, 2022. https://www.humanrestorationproject.org/writing/grading -gets-an-f-a-mathematicians-guide-to-the-absurdity-of-numerical -assessment

Smith, Jill M., and Ken Chih-Yan Sun. "Privileged American Families and Independent Academic Consultants They Employ." *Sociological Forum* 31 (2016): 159–80.

Sotardi, Valerie A. "Understanding Student Stress and Coping in Elementary School: A Mixed-Method, Longitudinal Study." *Psychology in the Schools* 53.7 (2016): 705–21.

Spera, Christopher. "Adolescents' Perceptions of Parental Goals, Practices, and Styles in Relation to Their Motivation and Achievement." *Journal of Early Adolescence* 26.4 (2006): 456–90.

Starch, Daniel, and Edward C. Elliott. "Reliability of the Grading of High-School Work in English." *The School Review* 20 (1912): 442–57.

State of Vermont's Agency of Education. "Flexible Pathways." Online resource. https://education.vermont.gov/student-learning/flexible-pathways

———. "Proficiency-Based Grading and Transcripts: Proficiency-Based Learning: Responding to Parent and Community Concerns." Online resource. https://education.vermont.gov/sites/aoe/files/documents/edu -proficiency-based-grading-and-transcripts-responding-to-parent-and -community-concerns.pdf

———. "Proficiency-Based Grading Practices and Transcripts." Online resource. https://education.vermont.gov/student-learning/proficiency -based-learning#grading-practices

———. "Proficiency-Based Learning Glossary." Online resource. https:// education.vermont.gov/sites/aoe/files/documents/edu-proficiency -based-learning-glossary_0.pdf

———. "Vermont Proficiency-Based Grading Practices." Online resource. https://education.vermont.gov/sites/aoe/files/documents/edu-vermont -proficiency-based-grading-practices.pdf

Steele, Claude M. *Whistling Vivaldi: How Stereotypes Affect Us and What We Can Do*. New York: Norton, 2010.

Stommel, Jesse. "Ungrading: An Introduction." jessestommel.com (blog). https://www.jessestommel.com/ungrading-an-introduction/

Stray, Christopher. "The Shift from Oral to Written Examination: Cambridge and Oxford 1700–1900." *Assessment in Education* 8 (2001): 33–50.

Suskie, Linda. *Assessing Student Learning: A Common Sense Guide*. 3rd ed. San Francisco: Jossey-Bass, 2018.

Tagg, John. *The Instruction Myth: Why Higher Education Is Hard to Change, and How to Change It*. New Brunswick, NJ: Rutgers UP, 2019.

Talbert, Robert. "Who Was Horace Mann? Much of Our Traditional Approach to Grading Comes Down to One Person." *Grading for Growth* (blog), December 5, 2022. https://gradingforgrowth.com/p/who-was -horace-mann?utm_source=%2Fsearch%2FMann&utm_medium =reader2

Tate, Allison Slater. "Colleges Welcome Growing Number of Homeschooled Students." *NBC News*, February 17, 2016. https://www.nbcnews.com /feature/college-game-plan/colleges-welcome-growing-number-home schooled-students-n520126

Toufexis, Anastasia. "Behavior: Report Cards Can Hurt You." *Time Magazine*, May 1, 1989. https://content.time.com/time/subscriber /article/0,33009,957572,00.html

Turgeon, Heather, and Julie Wright. *Generation Sleepless: Why Tweens and Teens Aren't Sleeping Enough and How We Can Help Them*. New York: TarcherPerigee, 2022.

Ulferts, Hannah. "Why Parenting Matters for Children in the 21st Century: An Evidence-Based Framework for Understanding Parenting and Its Impact on Child Development." *OECD Education Working Papers* 222. Organization for Economic Cooperation and Development's Directorate for Education, 2020.

University of California San Diego's Seventh College. "Welcome Prospective Students." https://seventh.ucsd.edu/about/prospective-students/index.html

University of Pennsylvania's Task Force on Student Psychological Health and Welfare. "Report." February 17, 2015. 1–8. https://almanac.upenn.edu/archive/volumes/v61/n23/pdf/task-force-psychological-health.pdf

Vermont General Assembly. H.181: "An Act Relating to Making Proficiency-based Learning and Proficiency-based Graduation Voluntary." 2021. https://legislature.vermont.gov/bill/status/2022/H.181

Volk, Steve. "The Tragedy of Madison Holleran and Suicides at Penn." *Philadelphia Magazine*, May 23, 2014. https://www.phillymag.com/news/2014/05/23/penn-suicides-madison-holleran/

Weis, Lois, and Kristin Cipollone. "'Class Work': Producing Privilege and Social Mobility in Elite US Secondary Schools." *British Journal of Sociology of Education* 34.5/6 (2013): 701–22.

Welner, Kevin G., and Prudence L. Carter. "Achievement Gaps Arise from Opportunity Gaps." In *Closing the Opportunity Gap: What America Must Do to Give Every Child an Even Chance*. Eds. Prudence L. Carter and Keven G. Welner. New York: Oxford University Press, 2013. 1–10.

Whisenhunt, Brooke L., Christie L. Cathey, Danae L. Hudson, and Lydia M. Needy. "Maximizing Learning while Minimizing Cheating: New Evidence and Advice for Online Multiple-Choice Exams." *Scholarship of Teaching and Learning in Psychology* 8 (2022): 140–53.

Worcester Polytechnic Institute. "Grade System." Online resource. https://www.wpi.edu/offices/registrar/policies-procedures/grade-system

Worcester Polytechnic Institute's Mental Health and Well-Being Task Force. "Initial Findings and Recommendations of the Mental Health and Well-Being Task Force, Phase One: Students." January 2022. 1–27. https://www.wpi.edu/sites/default/files/2022/01/19/WPI_MHWB_FindingsAndRecommendations_Phase1_2022.pdf

Yancey, Kathleen Blake. "Looking Back as We Look Forward: Historicizing Writing Assessment." *College Composition and Communication* 50 (1999): 483–503.

Zinn, Howard. *You Can't Be Neutral on a Moving Train: A Personal History of Our Times*. Boston: Beacon, 1994.

Index

academic freedom, 64

academic performance: Black parents' perspective on, 37–38; effect of opportunity gaps on, 71; effect of stereotype threat on, 81–82; gender differences, 74, 75, 76; "racialized," 79–81. *See also* grades; individual performance

academic standards, 63–64, 130–31; grade inflation and, 27–28. *See also* grading models, standards-based

achievement gaps, 67, 70–71, 73

achievement goals, 34, 35–36

ACT, preparatory classes, 39

administrators, xiii, 28, 71, 103, 108, 138, 139, 143, 144, 145–46

Advanced Placement (AP) courses, 37, 71, 79–80

agency model, of resiliency, 98–99

algebra, college-level, 74, 75

American College Health Association, National College Health Assessment for Fall 2022, 50–51

American Psychological Association (APA), 94, 96, 157n1

American School Counselor Association, 57

anxiety and anxiety disorders, xi, 17, 19–20, 48, 50, 55, 61, 82, 93, 153n2

appeals, of grades, 2

artificial intelligence (AI), generative, 21

arts disciplines, portfolio grading, 111–12

assessment: differentiated from evaluation, 1–2; in gradeless colleges, 130–31; grades as tools for, 1–3; plans, 115

attention impairment, 85

autonomy, 18, 20, 120

Bain, Ken, 14

Baltimore Mayor's Office for Children and Youth, 43–44

Battle Hymn of the Tiger Mother (Chua), 34

Bedi, Neil, 86

behaviorism, 15

Bell Curve, The (Herrnstein and Murray), 78

bell curves, 78

Big Ten, 73–76, 156n13

biological determinism, 78

Bird by Bird (Lamott), 123

Black students: out-of-school suspensions, 85–86; parents' perspectives on grades, 37–38; in segregated schools, 68–70. *See also* racial and social inequities, in education system

Buck, David, 109–10

Bushnell, Rebecca, 63

Butler, Ruth, 16–17

Cabrera, Alberto, 24

Calarco, Jessica McCrory, 80–81

Campbell, Corbin, 24

careers, college as preparation for, 36, 38–40, 41–42

Index

Index

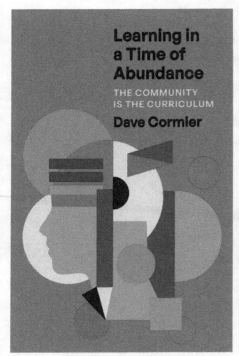
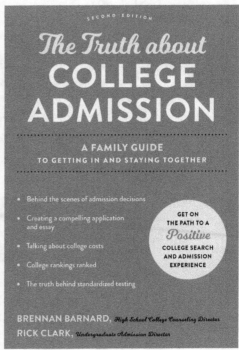